D0443147

ALSO BY JANINE SHEPHERD

Never Tell Me Never
Dare to Fly
Reaching for Stars
On My Own Two Feet
The Gift of Acceptance

DEFIANT

A Broken Body
Is Not A Broken Person

JANINE SHEPHERD

sounds true
BOULDER, COLORADO

Sounds True, Inc.
Boulder, CO 80306

Published 2016

Book design by Beth Skelley

Printed in Canada

Library of Congress Cataloging-in-Publication Data
Names: Shepherd, Janine, author.
Title: Defiant : a broken body is not a broken person / Janine Shepherd.
Description: Boulder, CO : Sounds True, 2017.
Identifiers: LCCN 2016009370 (print) | LCCN 2016028652 (ebook)
  | ISBN 9781622037100 | ISBN 9781622037117
Subjects: LCSH: Shepherd, Janine]—Health. | Quadriplegics
  Biography]—Australia. | Spinal cord]—Wounds and injuries—Patients
  Australia]—Biography. | Skiers]—Australia—Biography.
  | Crash injuries—Patients—Rehabilitation—Australia.
Classification: LCC RC406.Q33 S54 2017 (print) | LCC RC406.Q33 (ebook)
  | DDC 362.43092 [B]—dc23
LC record available at https://lccn.loc.gov/2016009370

eBook ISBN: 978-1-62203-711-7

10 9 8 7 6 5 4 3 2 1

Dedicated to my three beautiful children:
Annabel, Charlotte, and Angus.
And to David, my love.

And to all who heed the call of the defiant human spirit.

› PROLOGUE ‹

I was once given the most extraordinary gift. I lived in death for ten days. This was not the near-death experience so many people have described. There was no light at the end of the tunnel, no voices saying it was not yet my time. There were no religious images, no welcoming angels.

But I could move between dimensions at will. One moment, I was part of my body and in the physical plane; the next, I was in a distinctly spiritual one. Sometimes I was in both at once. The striking difference between them was that when I was in the physical dimension, I was aware of excruciating pain; while in the spiritual, I was detached from earthly concerns and painfree.

I was guided and nurtured by those who had traveled such a journey long before mine. There were no words spoken. Only thoughts. And those thoughts are difficult to recount. I experienced pure awareness. I was offered a choice: remain in this spiritual world or return to my physical body—a body seemingly broken beyond its ability to serve me. If I returned, I'd face unimaginable pain, incalculable physical and emotional loss, and my life would never be the same. This decision was mine alone to make.

I have always wondered why this "life-in-death" was unique to me. For years after my accident, I devoured books and stories of near-death experiences, or NDEs as we casually refer to them. I have yet to find anything that resembled my experience.

My family and the medical team in intensive care held anxious vigil as I clung to life. My internal bleeding was so profuse the doctors did not expect me to survive.

When I returned to my broken body—after ten days of confounding all attempts to stanch it—the internal bleeding had stopped.

I did not come back to my body to share my understanding of the afterlife: I returned to learn how to live fully. Once I'd made the choice to return, it proved far more useful to embrace my life in the present than to dream of ways to escape it.

And the gift? Those ten days in death, alternating between physical and ethereal planes, gave me a profound understanding of who I am. My purpose in life was revealed.

The gift of my death experience is a part of every cell of my being, every moment of every day. This is not something I believe; this is something I know.

There's one more thing I know: I am not my body, and you, dear reader, are not yours.

A broken body is *not* a broken person.

Janine Shepherd
Alta, Wyoming
March 2016

PART ONE
LIFE OR DEATH

Show me a way through this,
or show me a way out.

MAY 31, 1986

Castle Hill, near Sydney, Australia

"When will you be home?" Mum asked, as I rushed out the door and grabbed my bicycle.

"About ten tonight," I yelled back to her. My cycling partner, Chris, and I were already late, and everyone would be waiting for us.

I was dressed in riding shorts and a yellow jersey. I made a point of wearing brightly colored clothes when I biked on roads, as I'd already had a few scrapes with traffic. Riding home from the pool one day, I was passed by a truck whose driver didn't see me. I was forced into a ditch and suffered some nasty cuts and bruises. On another occasion, I was edged off the road and ended up with bruised ribs. Near misses such as these made me wary on busy thoroughfares and keen to be visible to drivers.

I pulled my helmet on, took a sip from my water bottle, and jumped on my bike. Chris pedaled close behind, working hard to keep up with my eager pace.

I always pushed myself to the limit, both physically and mentally. A natural athlete, I had represented my league and school teams at both state and national levels in a variety of sports, including softball and triathlons. Now, as the top performer in the Australian National Cross-Country Ski Team, I had found my sport. It was as if I'd been born for it. Training and competing in ski racing obsessed me in a way nothing else had. Cross-country skiing was my passion, and training events like that day's bike ride would help me start the upcoming season in top physical shape.

I waved goodbye to Mum and set off for the six-hour ride ahead. I was unusually tired that day; perhaps I'd been pushing myself too hard. The demanding training schedule and constant physical exertion were taking a toll. Only days before I had visited the doctor for tests to determine why I had skipped a few of my periods. I was diagnosed with "exercise amenorrhea," or lack of menstruation, common in female endurance athletes who overtrain. It was a confirmation that my body was under too much stress. I'd thought twice about even going on the ride with Chris and my friends, but the details and schedule had all been arranged, so I pushed aside my doubts and settled into my cycling rhythm.

There were about twenty of us on the ride, and as usual I was the only female. We called it the Rooster Ride because our destination was the Red Rooster Restaurant at the top of a mountain—the culmination of a grueling climb.

It was late morning before the group finally assembled and got rolling. The sun was beating down on us, so I took off my training jacket and packed it in my bag. When we reached the base of the mountains, we spread out, a natural response to the various levels of ability, desired intensity, and conditioning among the group of elite riders. Ever competitive, I rode near the front of the pack.

After an hour of pedaling flat terrain, we approached the foothills of the Blue Mountains. This was the part of the Rooster Ride I relished. I loved the hills. My training ethic and fierce competitiveness had earned me the nickname "Janine the Machine." Because I was focused, determined, and driven, I was on track to represent Australia in cross-country skiing at the 1988 Winter Olympics in Calgary. The Olympics are the ultimate dream for any athlete, and nothing was going to stand in my way. Nothing. Committed to making each training day count until then, I dug deep and pushed fatigue aside to tackle the challenging grades of this ride.

Once we were in the hills, the mood of the riders grew serious. As we climbed farther into the mountains, the temperature dropped, and the crisp mountain air burned my lungs with every deep breath. We put our heads down and concentrated on the grind of making it to the top. The incline made me redouble my efforts. As I reeled in and passed other riders, I could hear their labored breathing and see the strain in their faces. They were suffering. I pushed harder, spurred on to overtake each rider, one by one.

Approaching one of the final hills, I saw a lone cyclist ahead of me—John. I pushed to catch him and saw that he was flagging.

"Hey, mate! How you doing?" I asked, as I drew alongside, feigning a casual manner that belied the burning sensation in my legs. I didn't want him to see that I, too, was nearly spent.

"I'm starting to bonk," he replied. "I think I might get the train back to the city."

"Bonk" is a term used by athletes to describe the exhaustion that sets in when the body's energy stores begin to deplete—a long-distance athlete's nemesis.

We exchanged a few more words, and then I continued up the hill. There wasn't far to go, only a few miles, and then we would enjoy an afternoon of fine food at the Rooster. That was all the incentive I needed to keep going. I stood in the pedals and pumped my legs, determined to lead the group. I sucked in the cold air, lifted my head, and relished the sun shining on my face.

Then, everything went black.

› 2 ‹

1962–1986
Dural, New South Wales, Australia

I was the youngest of three girls in my family. Dad would have liked a son, but I was a tomboy who loved sports, so he wasn't disappointed.

I was involved in various athletic endeavors from an early age, especially track and field. I joined the Little Athletics Association of Australia, and each weekend was taken up with a competition of some sort. I'd enter as many different events as I could. I excelled at sprinting and by the age of ten had already accrued several wins in national championships. My aptitude became apparent, and my career as a serious competitor began.

As a consequence, our family traveled around Australia attending my state and national competitions. My two older sisters, Kim and Kelley, who tired of being dragged to these events, took to staying at home while one parent or the other shuttled me to and from my races.

Though I was given every opportunity to develop my natural sporting talent, Mum and Dad never pushed me. Participating in athletics was always my choice. They were proud of my achievements, but had I at any point chosen to stop competing, they would have supported my decision. I lived for my activities, and my happiest times as a child were running, playing a game of ball, or riding my skateboard.

My abiding interest in sporting competition met its first challenge when I entered high school, a time when socializing with peers took on a greater importance. Seeing that I was missing out on all the fun of being a teenager, I quit competing and turned my attention to building friendships. In retrospect, perhaps being so competitive at a young age burned me out by the time I reached high school. Nonetheless, my early athletic training gave me a foundation and skills that would serve me well later in life.

I settled into my studies, did well, and was accepted to study law at Macquarie University. Two years into my studies, the pull of sports took hold again. I changed course to pursue a degree in physical education and human movement studies at a different university. My new plan was to complete a postgraduate degree in exercise physiology, which at the time was offered only after completing a degree in a related field.

It was while I was at university that I became involved with my first serious boyfriend. Daven was a second-year law student I'd met through mutual friends. We'd bump into each other in the library on occasion, chatting nervously to deflect the awkward moments of a budding romance.

Daven plucked up the courage to ask me out on our first official date: a game of squash! I had been playing top-grade competition squash at the time, so Daven was a little taken aback when his date beat him on the courts. Undaunted, he asked me out again.

A Canadian, Daven donned his first pair of skis at age two and, by the time we met, had been a member of the Australian Alpine Ski Team (downhill racing) for several years. Like me, he was a natural athlete and excelled at sports. We spent our time together playing squash or on training runs through the campus. Daven and I became inseparable, our university lives revolving around both academics and athletics.

Daven rode his bike to school every day. He helped me buy my first racing bike, and from that moment on, I rode to class every day, too. Cycling was an excellent off-season training regimen to prepare both lungs and legs for skiing.

Around that time, triathlons—swimming, cycling, and running races combined in one event—became popular in Australia. Daven and I started to train for competition on the triathlon circuit. With a background in running and my recent foundation in cycling, I needed only to work on my swimming to round out the three-event complement. After working on my swimming technique and in-water endurance, I started to do well in the shorter triathlons. Before long I won the New South Wales State Championship and, with it, my first treasured competition prizes: a racing bike and an oversized trophy.

I was proud, but my enjoyment of this and all other athletic endeavors paled in comparison to my love for skiing. Although I had taken up the sport relatively late—in my teenage years for downhill and even later for cross-country—my background in endurance events was the ideal preparation for this demanding and grueling sport, which consumed me. Daven was growing tired of downhill racing and the crowds at the resorts. Together we relished the freedom of getting out on cross-country ski tracks that wound through peaceful forest trails.

I possessed the ideal physical attributes for cross-country ski racing: the aerobic endurance of a marathon runner complemented by arm and leg strength. Once I mastered the "skate" technique, unique to cross-country skiing, I began to compete at a top level in this new-to-me circuit.

Given that my interest in the sport developed so late, most of the other skiers hadn't heard of me when I entered my first race in the small town of Cabramurra. It was a lead-up event to the state championships, and much to everyone's surprise, I went on to win by a wide margin, beating the top contenders. In fact, my time was comparable to those recorded in the Scandinavian nations that consistently dominate Nordic ski racing—something never before achieved by an Australian skier.

Training for both improved technique and greater endurance, I soon qualified as a candidate for the Australian National Ski Team. I would have been satisfied with selection for the B team—competitors in the lower-tier races—so I was thrilled when I was slated for the A team. This made me eligible for the highest-level national and international races and qualified me for an extended overseas competition tour.

The cross-country skiing circuit consists of two main events, the Europa Cup and the more prestigious World Cup. To compete in the World Cup, skiers had to record certain minimum qualifying times by gender. No woman from Australia had posted qualifying times—in fact, my country had no females on the World Cup circuit. I was keen to change that. After a few qualifying races, I scored results that secured my eligibility for the World Cup competition. Soon I received the coveted endorsement of the Australian Ski Federation, ranking me at the most elite national level.

My key race results were more than promising, including winning a 25-kilometer major race in Italy, the Dolomitenlauf—an event that I'd entered purely as a training run. My World Cup results were improving with each event, and the experience of competing against the world's best skiers began to pay off. By the end of the season, I was confident in my ability and excited at the prospect of representing Australia in the 1988 Olympics.

I became friendly with women athletes representing other teams on the World Cup circuit, especially the Canadians. The Canadian Ski Team was one of the best in the world and the hosts of the upcoming Olympics in Calgary. They traveled with an entourage of assistants, doctors, coaches, physiotherapists, and ski technicians—advantages well beyond the budget of the Australians.

One day after we finished racing, the Canadian coach, Marty Hall, invited me to join him and the girls on the team for pizza. We spent hours talking and eating while I told them about life in Australia. Later, at an awards ceremony, Marty asked me about my plans for the future.

"I'll go back to university and finish my studies before returning to Europe next year with the team," I replied.

He gave that some thought. "You know, if you really want to make it in competitive skiing, you'll have to put your studies on hold until the Olympics are over. Training logistics aren't so complicated for the Australian men's team—there are more of them—and they travel together and work with one another for support. But you're the lone female racer. Australia doesn't even have a women's team, and without the benefit of team dynamics, it will be nearly impossible for you to break into the top level of women competitors."

"I hear you, Marty, but if I want to compete, what choice do I have?"

"I'm convinced you can make it on the world stage of female ski racers," he said. "You have what it takes, but your only chance is to join up with a women's team that competes at that level. What I'm saying is . . . "

He went on to make me a stunning offer: the opportunity to train as part of the Canadian team for the season leading up to the Olympics. If I accepted, I would meet up with the team in the United States in November and travel with them as an ex-officio member. I would enjoy full use of their world-class facilities and resources.

I couldn't believe my ears. This was the opportunity of a lifetime!

"Marty, I'd love to! I want to show the world that Australians are competitive and a skiing force to be reckoned with, even if we are on the other side of the world!"

"I believe you can do that, Janine, but you need the support the Canadian team can provide. And there's no time to waste. The Olympics are just around the corner."

Marty was right. Never one to hesitate, my decision was made: I would join my new Canadian teammates as soon as possible. I made the necessary arrangements to return home and defer my studies until after the Calgary Olympics.

By the time I made it back to Australia in March, I arranged a transfer to the University of Canberra so that I could be closer to the ski fields and the Australian Institute of Sport. In May I attended a training camp where the Australian ski team was tested for aerobic endurance and strength. My results were way above any of the other girls and bested most of the males as well. My oxygen uptake, or VO2 max (a prerequisite for success in any endurance sport), was the highest they had ever tested for a female. My body fat percentage was so low that it was less than most of the males.

With this validation of my physical capacity and the prospect of training with the Canadians, I felt the planets aligning for my Olympic bid. Everything I had done in my life—the countless hours training, the demanding races, the suffering—had prepared me for my chance to compete among the world's top ski racers. With so much to look forward to in the year leading up to the Olympics, I threw myself into my studies and my training, but I couldn't wait to get back on the snow.

> 3 <

MAY 31, 1986

Westpac Rescue Helicopter Landing
at Prince Henry Hospital

"What have we got here?" asked the hospital's receiving doctor.

"Twenty-four-year-old female, transferred from Blue Mountains Hospital in Katoomba."

"What are her vital signs?"

"Multiple trauma, internal bleeding, fractured L1 and T10 paraparesis, frank hematuria, pelvic damage. Heart rate: 90. Blood pressure: 96 over 65 and falling. Still in shock. She may need more fluid. She's had two units of blood, one unit Hartmann's, and 25 mg pethidine. Looks like you'll be with this one for a while."

"Thanks. We'll take it from here."

"Good luck. I wouldn't plan on getting any sleep tonight!"

With that, the helicopter first responders departed, and the hospital emergency team sprang into action.

"Nurse, let's get moving. What's her current status?"

"I can't find a pulse . . . still trying to get a read on her blood pressure."

"Come on, let me try. Blood pressure has dropped: it's 40 over *nothing*. Move! We've got to get her out of here. Phone intensive care, and tell them we've got a hot one!"

I shivered uncontrollably. I was aware of gripping pain, like a vice tightening with each tortured breath. I heard voices but barely made out the words. *Where was I?* The world around me was bewildering. A tube in my mouth reached down into my stomach and made me nauseous. I lifted my hands and blinked to clear my vision. Through a blur, I saw a maze of tubes attached to my arms, which felt like lead. There was something cold on my chest. I tried to raise my head to see what it was, but a searing jolt shot through me, forcing my head to crash back down. *What was that?*

Through the fog of shock, I began to sort it out. There was something encircling my neck, locking it in place. I could hear a strange, mechanical beep from above me. I strained to see what it might be, but I was pinned to the hard bed.

I blinked and attempted to hold my eyes open to focus. Stark white light struck my face with such intensity it forced me to close my eyes again. Gasping, I reached for whatever was smothering me, some sort of mask covering my face. I wanted to remove it, but my wrist was gripped in a tight lock.

What's happening to me? Where am I? I must be dreaming. All of it was so confusing. Like a nightmare, fragments of memories emerged, snapshots of faces: my parents, my friends. *This is all so crazy! I'm losing control.*

"Someone help me! Please . . . help . . . me!" I screamed, but I had no voice.

I tried to move but was overwhelmed by an electrifying pain in my back. With growing dread, it dawned on me that I couldn't move my legs. I couldn't even feel them. Panic consumed me. Again I tried to lift my arms but was held down by a weight I couldn't overcome. Excruciating pain enveloped my body, making me retch and gag on the tube in my throat. I was a person who was defined by athletic prowess, endurance, and strength, yet I was unable to move my head. Janine the Machine was helpless.

Somebody must be able to hear me. Mum? Dad?

I was suffocating! Something covered my mouth. I struggled to find the wherewithal to pull it away, but this time I was stopped and heard, "Janine, it's all right. It's oxygen. You need the mask to breathe." Someone was with me, though I couldn't place the voice.

"Pl-please . . . off . . . " I strained to speak even a few syllables with my parched mouth, desperate to be understood and to understand. Nausea washed over me again, as I struggled and failed to maintain consciousness.

My eyes fluttered open again. Someone stood above me. I realized the oxygen mask had been adjusted, and I gulped fresh air. I opened my mouth to speak, but no words came out.

"Can you say your name?" That voice again. *Who was speaking to me?*

"Y-yes," I stammered. "J-nin . . . "

"Do you know where you are?"

What does she mean?

"Janine, you have to answer. Can you tell me what happened to you?"

Why was she persisting? I was too confused to piece it all together.

"Janine, you've had an accident. You were run over riding your bike."

The words had no meaning, no context. *If I close my eyes, all this will go away. I will wake up and be home in my bed.*

A country road, a lone cyclist, and a reckless driver combined to create a moment in time that changed a life forever.

On the day of the accident, my parents had been out looking at gardens, gathering ideas for the dream house they were building. When they arrived home, the phone was ringing. It was my friend John.

"Janine has been in an accident," he told them, the anxiety in his voice apparent.

"How serious?" Dad asked.

"She's okay, but you need to get to the hospital as soon as possible."

Mum and Dad sensed there was more to it than John was letting on. Sensitive to the fact that my parents faced a two-hour drive up the mountains to where I was being treated, John thoughtfully lied and assured them I was okay. They rushed to depart, concerned but with no idea what was in store for them once they got to the hospital.

A young doctor on exchange from the UK met them when they arrived. He was a newly minted intern in his first hospital placement, and he had the task of breaking the news to Mum and Dad—his unpleasant indoctrination to real-life emergency medicine.

At nearly the exact moment Mum and Dad arrived, my blood pressure dropped precipitously. It was imperative that the doctors stabilize it before they could even consider transferring me to a facility better suited to handle my injuries. Units of blood were flown up from Sydney to provide the supply I needed. My internal bleeding was profuse and showed no signs of abating. I ended up losing more than five quarts—the amount someone my size would hold.

Along with the drop in blood pressure, this uncontrolled bleeding alarmed the attending physicians. Until they could get ahead of the blood loss, my survival was in jeopardy. My other injuries were serious, but they would have to wait.

My parents walked into the doctors' chaotic and terrifying struggle to save my life.

"Is she going to be okay?" Mum asked, her voice wavering with the awareness that things were far more serious than she'd assumed.

"It's too early to tell. It was a bad accident. We suspect she has spinal damage, but there are also a lot of internal injuries," a doctor told her.

"But she's going to be okay!" Mum demanded, now almost pleading.

"In her favor, she is strong and young, but there's a lot of damage. We're doing everything we can, but we first have to get her stabilized and may have to fly her to Sydney."

Mum fell silent in shock.

"Mrs. Shepherd, we can give you something to calm you down."

"No, thank you." If ever she needed a clear head, Mum knew it was now.

The medical staff fought to stabilize my blood pressure and to stanch the internal bleeding, but the attending physicians saw that my deteriorating condition required specialized care beyond the limits of what this small-town hospital could provide.

"Mr. and Mrs. Shepherd, Janine's condition has become critical. She requires delicate emergency surgery. We are coordinating a life-flight transfer to a hospital in Sydney better equipped to handle your daughter's injuries."

There wasn't time to console or explain. The staff was in triage mode, and my parents had to accept what scant updates they were given.

Braced as best as possible to avoid further damage to my neck and spine, I was loaded aboard the life-flight helicopter destined for Westmead Hospital. As the life-threatening nature of my injuries grew more apparent en route, the helicopter medical team decided to divert to a facility with a specialized spinal unit: Prince Henry.

Sick with dread and largely in silence, Mum and Dad drove to where they'd been instructed, Westmead. They arrived to confusion. The staff there had no idea who I was, not to mention where I might be. After a number of panicked calls and what must have seemed an eternity, my parents learned of the diversion to Prince Henry. Already distraught and operating on almost no information about my welfare, they soldiered on for another hour drive to Prince Henry.

Mum and Dad now had to find a hospital they had never heard of, in a place they'd never been, all the while overcome with fear and dread for the life and well-being of their child. To make matters worse, they had to drive in torrential rain. Their anxiety rose near the point of being unbearable. It didn't help that on arrival they were ushered into a ward to face another agonizing wait while the doctors in the ER battled to stabilize my condition.

I was still losing blood as quickly as it was being transfused. Pressure readings remained perilously low. As my condition deteriorated, a team of neurosurgeons, orthopedic physicians, and intensive care attendants assembled and began round-the-clock duty. The anesthetist, Dr. Denis Kerr, was a member of this team, and it was he who briefed Mum and Dad on my condition.

"Mr. and Mrs. Shepherd," Dr. Kerr began, "Janine has broken her neck as well as her back." He hesitated before resuming his update, "But that is not our main concern. She has serious internal bleeding, which we aren't yet able to stop. We don't know exactly where it is coming from."

Dr. Kerr was merciful and didn't specifically mention the suspected spinal cord damage. Although it was serious, it was not the most life-threatening issue I faced at that moment. Dr. Kerr knew my parents had to come to grips with the fact that I might not survive. "We're having trouble stabilizing her blood pressure because of her blood loss. We are doing everything we can; however, you need to prepare for the worst."

The night dragged on, and the wait between updates was almost unbearable for Mum and Dad. The hospital staff arranged for them to spend the night in nearby nurses' quarters. Numb with exhaustion and sick with dread, Mum and Dad turned in for what was the longest night of their lives. They tossed and turned, consumed with worry. The hours dragged on. Then, in the early morning, Mum heard a voice echoing down the hall.

"Mr. Shepherd? Mrs. Shepherd?" The voice was insistent.

Mum sat up in bed, terrified at the prospect of hearing news they dreaded.

"Yes, yes, we're awake!" my father said, his heart in his throat, as he ran to meet the nurse at the doorway.

"The doctor asked if you could come to the ward straightaway."

"What's happened?"

"It's all right," she reassured him. "Janine is calling for you. The doctor thinks it would help her if you came right away."

"Thank God," Mum said.

My parents wept with relief when they heard the news that there was still a chance I'd survive.

><

As the days passed, my medical team felt no such moments of elation. The bleeding continued unabated, confounding the doctors. For me, time seemed dreamy and suspended, as I drifted in and out of consciousness, while my family and a few close friends maintained vigil, praying for a miracle.

After three days, and still wearing the clothes he'd arrived in, my father drove home for supplies. While Mum was alone at the hospital, my condition took a turn for the worse. The doctors took her aside: the constant bleeding was beyond their control. Being told in essence to prepare for my death, Mum would later recall that day as the most devastating of her long vigil.

Still, while the doctors fought relentlessly to save me, I was on another plane fighting my own spiritual battle. On one side was the physical part of me, pinned to the bed in ICU and struggling to survive. But the other part of me was detached and free, watching the goings-on in the ward from a separate dimension, an observer to events as they unfolded.

I was in a "place" where I didn't need eyes to see. Words were unnecessary, too. Here, I was able to perceive messages from beyond the familiar physical world. I was not alone, and although I didn't know the people supporting me, I understood and accepted without question that I was somehow being guided through my experience and that any decisions to be made were mine alone. Their message to me was unequivocal: there was still time to return to my body and live out my life, but it was my choice—and one I had to make now.

In this new place, I understood that my physical self was close to death. I watched as my body suffered agony. Even if by some miracle of medicine—one that had thus far eluded the best doctors in Sydney—my life could be saved, my mangled body was far too damaged to serve me any longer as an athlete.

I found myself in a holding pattern, a netherworld between death and life. My body had been both my vehicle and the focus of my identity. If I were no longer Janine the Machine, then who was I? Should I return to my broken body and the possibility of life in a wheelchair, with all the limitations of yet unknown disabilities? How could I choose a future bereft of the physical joy that had defined me as an elite athlete? Faced with the prospect of a life forever altered by my injuries, I felt compelled to let go.

Yet I didn't. Something held me back, an inexorable pull that would not release my spirit. As much as I willed myself free of the constraints of my broken body, I was unable to do so.

Then I realized why: Dad had joined Mum at my bedside. I felt the pull of his presence and love. He had my hand in his, and his words entered my awareness: "Please God, don't let her go. Take my strength and give it to Janine."

I made my choice, and with a swiftness and completeness that the medical team to this day cannot account for, my internal bleeding stopped.

› 4 ‹

TEN DAYS AFTER THE ACCIDENT
Prince Henry Hospital

"Dad . . . " I opened my eyes to see my father's face illuminated by the sterile bright lights of the ICU ward.

His familiar voice was loving, soothing. "I'm right here, sweetheart. I won't leave."

"Wh-where's Mum?" My muffled words from under the oxygen mask were barely audible.

"She's here, right beside you," Dad answered, his voice wavering, as he strained to keep his words coherent while choked with emotion.

"Help me . . . "

"Hush. Don't try to talk. The doctors are looking after you. Everything will be all right. Mum and I are with you, and we're not leaving."

I didn't know it then, but the last ten days had been the fight of my life and *for* my life. Once I had chosen to return to my broken body, the fight played out in a different but no less daunting arena. When the profuse internal bleeding had miraculously stopped, my parents and caretakers could relax, knowing that I would at least survive. But for me, the struggle took on a different dimension: returning to my body was a physical challenge far greater than any I had ever faced as an athlete.

The only respite from the relentless agony was provided by the morphine drip attached to my arm. It pumped the powerful narcotic through my body, enabling me to drift off to sleep. As time passed and it started to wear off, I was forced awake—groggy and bathed in perspiration. I then had to endure unimaginable agony until my next dose.

With the immediate threat to my life gone, my doctors shifted their focus to assess the damage to my spinal cord. The initial medical finding was that I had broken my back and my neck. X-rays revealed I had six broken vertebrae, the most severe fracture being L1, in my lower back. With these injuries came the likelihood of significant spinal cord damage and the question of whether I would ever walk again.

These weren't the only unknowns. Each time Mum and Dad received updates from my doctors, the list of injuries grew. There were fractures in my right arm and to my collarbone. I had five broken ribs on my left side and several broken bones in my feet. I had also sustained serious head injuries: my scalp had required stitching to reattach it because the force of the impact had peeled skin back at the forehead and across my skull.

Contusions to my kidneys—bruises caused by the trauma—stained my urine with blood. Extensive lacerations to my abdominal area and my right leg were still filled with gravel and grit because no one yet had the luxury of time to clean and dress these wounds. The focal point of impact—where the truck struck my lower back and buttocks—was covered with a massive hematoma. Hip and leg muscles had been torn away. There wasn't much of my body that hadn't been damaged, and it remained unclear which injuries would be recoverable and which would remain chronic or even disabling.

I became oblivious to the array of medical paraphernalia that had become an essential part of my existence. The suffocating face mask was removed, but that was short-lived relief because the nasogastric (in my nose) and orogastric (in my mouth) tubes remained. The tube in my mouth reached into my stomach, to decompress the digestive tract, helping to stave off the urge to vomit and encouraging the flow of blood to damaged areas of my spinal cord. As if these unrelenting discomforts weren't enough, an overarching frustration was my being forced to lie on a thin, hard "bed"—a slab, really, designed to stabilize my spine. And I was naked, with only a sheet draped over me in a considerate but futile effort to preserve some degree of dignity.

I still had heart-monitoring ECG sensors taped to my chest. Intravenous tubes for the blood and saline drips were anchored to one arm, while the other was kept immobile by a plaster cast. I also continued to rely on a catheter to drain body wastes and toxins from my bladder.

Head movement was restricted by a brace—it was still too early to determine whether the break in my neck was stable, so to avoid the threat of paralysis, it had to remain immobilized.

Thus disabled, I relied on other people's observations to form my perceptions of the ward. I found I could absorb a certain amount of information despite the fuzziness caused by the meds, but my full mental capacity had yet to return. Piecing together overheard snippets of conversation, I learned that I was in the intensive care unit reserved for serious trauma victims. Normally, spinal injuries were treated in a special unit in the hospital, but the multiple life-threatening injuries I had sustained meant I was far from out of the woods and required the constant vigilance of the ICU.

The rules and regulations in the ICU were a lot stricter than in other wards of the hospital. To avoid strain on both the patients and the overworked staff, only immediate family and a few close friends were allowed brief visits, limited to two people at a time. Although Mum and Dad were permitted to stay longer, even they were not permitted in the ICU during critical procedures.

News of my accident was reported on the radio, newspapers, and television, so many of my friends heard about it. Later I was told they'd waited outside the ICU for their turn to see me. Some were persistent enough to succeed in getting through the ICU gatekeepers, though sadly I have no recollection of seeing anyone except Mum, Dad, and the constant stream of medical aides, nurses, and doctors tending to my needs.

Even as I made halting progress toward healing, it seemed there was always some new threat or setback. The hematoma on my back and buttocks, which otherwise might have been taken as incidental, caused the medical staff a great deal of anxiety. The pooled blood created a serious risk of developing into a clot. If that broke loose and entered my bloodstream, it could prove fatal. To guard against that possibility, the medical staff treated the wounded area with ultrasound twice a day, hoping to encourage reabsorption of the blood and reduction of the swelling.

A related risk for an immobilized patient with so many injuries is blood clotting in some less obvious part of the body. Even a small clot could travel in the bloodstream, and if the resulting embolism lodged in an artery, it could block blood flow to a vital organ. To guard against this, the medical team regularly turned me onto my side to encourage the blood to circulate. Though this process proved painful, I can't begin to describe the incredible relief for me to be off my back and not lying on the hematoma that tormented me, even if just for a moment.

My most grave injuries, my back and neck breaks in particular, required special care over and above the more basic palliative treatments for trauma wounds. With the extent of injury still undetermined, it was imperative that my spine be kept in perfect alignment during the rotation process necessary for good circulation. Given the risk of permanent damage to the spinal cord from even a small tweak, extra precaution was taken to ensure that I was turned with the utmost care. The drill was that two orderlies would stand at my side: one would brace my neck and head; the other, my trunk. On the count of three, they synchronized their actions to rotate me and ensure my spine and neck stayed rigid.

For Mum and Dad, the waiting game continued. They often took solace in a small chapel on the hospital grounds, with views of the Pacific Ocean. Next to the chapel was a wishing well, where Dad would often toss a coin and whisper a prayer that our nightmare would end so we could return to some semblance of a normal family.

I clung to life in my own confused and nightmarish world, unaware of what my parents were going through. My world was focused on addressing the constant pain—anything else was inconsequential. I was given information on what the medical staff deemed a need-to-know basis, which meant I wasn't told much at all. The doctors advised my parents to keep the growing inventory of my injuries to themselves and to answer questions only when I asked. My caregivers knew this would give me the best chance of coping with a situation that could overwhelm someone in my compromised state.

Each day I lived in a fog. Everything seemed distant and unreal. Often I'd imagine that all I had to do was close my eyes and I would wake up in my own bedroom, ready to go on a run. Perhaps this state of delirium was a coping mechanism, but it allowed me to get through each day and to hope that things might not be as bad as they appeared.

It was in my nature to ask questions, and I did whenever I was able.

"Dr. Kerr," I'd say, struggling not to slur my words in my half-drugged state, "when will I be able to go home? I have to get back to my training."

"Honestly, Janine," he'd say gently, "don't think about that now. All you need to do is rest so that we can get you better, okay?" And with that vague encouragement, he left me to wonder at my prospects for recovery.

As I made modest gains in strength and awareness, I grew increasingly concerned about my legs and feet. I constantly tried to move them, an effort that remained fruitless. And I still had no sensation whatsoever in my lower body.

Taking stock of the injuries and symptoms, I couldn't fathom what they all meant. It dawned on me that my injuries were more extensive than I had feared. Would I ski again? Would I walk again? Would I become a prisoner to my yet-to-be determined disabilities?

Such obsessive thoughts began to torment me in a relentless and dark way. An indescribable sense of dread comes from waking up in a hospital bed paralyzed and unable to piece together the sequence of events that brought you there. In the cloying darkness of night, my obsessive thought process was still more terrible. Time seemed suspended in a waking nightmare. My dark thoughts were amplified by the ever-present state of disconnect between my life before the accident and the reality I was now living. Like so many accident victims, I refused to accept that this could be happening to me.

To escape the nightmare, I would close my eyes and drift off, dreaming of things as they were before the accident, and as I awakened, visualizing that they would be that way again. At times when the fog of the drugs lifted, my mind was still able to control what I envisioned as my destiny. The competitive athlete in me was not about to give up.

› 5 ‹

Determined to have a say in my recovery, I embraced working with my medical team. Checkups from neurosurgeons, orthopedic physicians, and rehabilitation specialists relieved the boredom of lying in a hospital bed and being unable to move. I took an active and keen interest in my progress. I wasn't satisfied to be a "patient." Instead, I demanded to know everything about my condition, from the medications they were prescribing to the results of each test.

When I was transferred from the ICU to the acute spinal ward, I shared the space with five other patients. Days passed in a monotony of routine, until something miraculous happened: lying in bed, once again trying to move my legs, I was excited by the smallest twitch in my right foot. Surely this was a sign that I would be walking—and skiing—again!

Everyone in the ward was as thrilled as I was with this development, and this flicker of progress encouraged my doctors as well. I fully believed that I was now on my way to regaining full use of my legs. This measure of hope spurred me on and helped me to disregard the other symptoms that were not so positive: I remained numb from the buttocks down. Still I was undaunted. Each day as I lay in bed, eyes closed, I would focus all my energy on moving just my feet. Despite the fact that I had no physical confirmation of movement, I was convinced I was making progress.

Instead, my recovery took a turn for the worse. The response in my feet began to diminish, until I lost the ability to elicit any movement at all. My neurologist, Dr. Blum, had hoped that my incremental neurological improvements would continue, so the unexplained regression was baffling and alarming. He ordered tests to ascertain the reason for my setback.

I was taken for a myelogram, a test that determines nerve signal continuity. When I was first told about the test, I had yet to grasp how dire the situation was. I still believed it was only a matter of time before I could go home and begin training again. I was wheeled to the X-ray department, unaware of the challenges ahead of me. The myelogram would prove to be an excruciating procedure.

First I was transferred to an even harder bed (something I wouldn't have thought possible), which was then tilted to give the technicians access to my back. Out of the corner of my eye, I could see the staff preparing the equipment. They began by inserting an oversized hypodermic syringe into my spine to anesthetize the area. Then they used an even larger needle to inject dye into my spinal cavity. A throbbing sensation shot through my back as the dye dispersed. The bed was then tilted more, to force the dye to penetrate the full length of my spinal cord.

I then had to endure an inordinate length of time in this position to allow for a series of X-rays to determine whether the dye made its way along the cord unobstructed. If not, that almost certainly meant a blockage, which implied impingement on the spinal cord and, with it, a loss of neurological function.

This awful procedure—besides being uncomfortable—left me with dreadful side effects: a splitting headache, a metallic taste in my mouth, and an overwhelming sense of nausea. I was never so glad to be back in the familiar surroundings of the spinal ward, which had now become my home. Exhausted, all I wanted was to close my eyes, drift off to sleep, and await the findings.

The next morning Mum and Dad were at my bedside when Dr. Blum made an unscheduled visit. I sensed he was not his usual cheery self.

"We've been looking over the results of Janine's myelogram," he said, "and I'm afraid it doesn't look good. She suffered what we call a 'burst fracture' in her back, meaning there are a lot of bony fragments compressing her spine. She'll need surgery to decompress the spine and remove the fragments, with a bone graft to make the spinal column rigid again."

"When will you operate?" Mum asked.

"Well, it's important we do it sooner rather than later."

"Do we have any choice?"

"Unfortunately, no. If we do the procedure, there is a small chance that Janine might walk again. But if we don't, she will almost certainly end up in a wheelchair. And I have to let you know that this is a serious surgery involving a delicate part of the body, so there are significant risks."

I tried to comprehend what Dr. Blum was saying. Phrases like "no choice," "might walk again," and "significant risk" sounded surreal. Until then, I had believed in my progress and that I would soon return to my life before the accident. What did this new development portend? For the first time, I came face to face with the dreadful reality of my injuries, and it made me ill, to the point of delirium and the all-too-familiar nausea.

Dr. Blum took my parents outside to discuss the details of the operation. A wave of panic washed over me. "Please, someone, help me!" I screamed. I began to shake uncontrollably. The nurse on duty rushed to my bed and called for assistance. The moment they turned me on my side, I vomited violently.

The nurse then washed my face with soothing cold water, hoping to assuage my panic. I was exhausted and overwhelmed by the news from the test. After she gave me an injection to calm me, I lay in bed, staring at the ceiling. Until this turn of events, I had been unable, or unwilling, to grasp the severity of the situation. Now I began to ask the inevitable questions: *Why me? Why has this happened? What good could come of this?* Tears rolled down my cheeks as I closed my eyes and waited for the sedative to take effect.

The operation was scheduled for exactly six weeks after my accident. Initially, the doctors had forecast eight weeks of immobility when I first arrived at the hospital, so I'd been steadily counting down with each passing day. Now, with only two weeks left to go, the prognosis had changed to be far less hopeful. After the operation, I would have to spend at least an additional twelve weeks in bed. How could I endure that? Maybe I was no longer an aspiring Olympic ski racer, but I was still a hopeful twenty-four-year-old woman with a full life ahead. Dr. Blum's foreboding words made me despair for my future.

Although I had a general understanding of the surgical procedure that would fix the fractured vertebra, the finer details were still uncertain. It didn't help to know that until the surgical team opened me up and assessed the damage, both the exact nature of the repair and the outcome were anyone's guess.

Not surprisingly, I was unable to sleep the night before the operation. Not even the drugs offered any relief. I knew this was a crucial operation: one small mistake would mean irreparable damage and the likelihood of a wheelchair-bound future. *What happens if the operation goes wrong? My world is the life of an athlete—if I no longer have that, then what?* Never in my life had I been so frightened. The clinical sounds and smells of the ward served as grim reminders of the reality of my situation. It was an agonizing night.

The next morning, the staff began preparing me for the operation. Mum and Dad were at my side by the time the orderlies arrived. I was given an injection meant to calm my nerves, but instead, it made me shiver uncontrollably. Things were off to a rough start. My parents kissed me and reassured me they would be there when the operation was over. Despite their courage, I could see the anguish in their eyes. They were afraid, too.

"Don't worry. I'll be okay," I said with a jaunty thumbs-up and a smile to hide my fear. It was my turn to be strong.

› 6 ‹

Coming out of the blackness, I recognized the bright lights of the ICU. Struggling to take a breath, I was stopped by a sharp, piercing sensation in my chest. I instinctively reached to my side and realized that my entire chest had been bandaged, making it a struggle to draw a full breath. I wrapped my left arm around my chest, pressing firmly on my side, which helped slightly, but I could still manage only a few small sips of air at a time.

I was drowsy and vaguely nauseous. The anesthesia had yet to wear off. I strained to keep my eyes open. Through the blur, I could make out the faces of Mum and Dad. With great effort, I reached toward them.

"Hi, sweetheart. It's all over," Mum reassured me as she took my hand. I tried to respond, but it hurt to speak.

"Dr. Blum said everything went well. Try to get some rest."

I tried to take a few more sips of air, pressing my arm even harder to my side. The nurse came over, and I tried again to speak, this time managing a whisper. "I'm so sore . . . "

"Janine, it's all right. It's normal."

I tightened my grip on my side. I would later learn that to access the damaged part of my spine, the surgeons had to cut me halfway around my trunk, from my lower abdomen to my upper back.

"You have to be careful not to move too much," the nurse said, as she pointed to a tube protruding from my stomach. "You have a drain for the incision, which needs to stay for a few days."

As she left, two orderlies arrived. Their job was to turn the patients to avoid bedsores, but surely they couldn't be about to turn me, so soon after surgery? I could hardly tolerate the pain of lying there—so the mere thought of being turned was unbearable. My chest throbbed with each shallow, forced breath, and my eyes widened with fear as the orderlies approached my bed.

"How are you doing, love? Ready to be turned?" Without waiting for a reply, they positioned themselves on either side of me.

"Please don't move me. I'm too sore," I whimpered.

"Sorry, love, but we have to—regulations, you know."

"Please, can't you miss just this once? Please . . . "

"Well, okay. I guess it'll be all right. We'll be back in two hours anyway." They moved on to the next bed.

What a relief! I closed my eyes and tried to think of anything but the unrelenting pain in my chest. I wasn't sure how much time had passed when I opened my eyes to see Dr. Blum by my bedside. I was still groggy from the anesthetic but pleased to see his smiling face.

"Well then, young lady, how are you feeling? A bit sore they tell me."

That was an understatement.

"Let's see if you have any movement in your feet now."

I closed my eyes, and with every ounce of strength I could muster, I imagined myself moving my feet. I was sure I could sense them shift ever so slightly.

"Did you see that?" I said, with as much enthusiasm as I could muster in my foggy state. "I think they moved a bit!"

"I think you're right," said Dr. Blum, smiling.

"I'll be able to ski again. Won't I?"

Deftly sidestepping my question, he replied, "I'm pleased with the operation. It couldn't have gone better. I'll be back tomorrow to check on you. Keep up the good work." He smiled again and wiggled one of my feet affectionately before he left the ward.

It couldn't have gone better. That was all I needed to affirm my conviction that I'd soon be leaving the hospital and getting back to my old life. Though I had lots of catching up to do, maybe the Olympics in Calgary were still within reach. I closed my eyes and drifted off with images of skiing in my mind. For the first time in a long while, I found peace in sleep.

"Good morning, Janine. How are we today? I'm Jenny, your physiotherapist."

A physiotherapist? What could she possibly want? No way I could get out of this bed, much less even think about exercise.

"Your lungs and chest have been through quite a bit of trauma during the operation. We need to keep them free of fluids or any infections. We have to give them some exercise."

She handed me a strange contraption—a tube with some little plastic balls inside—and instructed me to blow into it as forcefully as I could. The goal was to keep those balls floating in the tube for as long as possible with each exhalation.

She had to be kidding! I could barely draw a full breath, let alone expel it forcefully enough to make those little balls rise. Holding the device, which I learned was called an inspirometer, I summoned my best effort and tried my first deep breath. It was of no use because the stitches in my chest and back pulled with a searing reminder of my incision. I exhaled a pathetic puff into the tube.

"Come on, Janine. You've got to try and lift the balls. Have another go."

I tried and tried but still the balls didn't budge. Satisfied I'd given my best effort, Jenny moved me on to a new form of torture: forced coughing. *Can this get any worse?* I tried to appease her with a few feeble wheezes so as not to jar my sutures, but I wasn't really coughing.

Therapist visits like Jenny's became a routine designed to ensure my lungs stayed clear and didn't collapse. It was a rigorous and sometimes agonizing grind, but one I disciplined myself to work through. I knew the sooner I could get those balls to rise, the sooner I could go home.

After seven days in the ICU, I was pronounced stable enough to return to the spinal ward, where my fellow patients greeted me enthusiastically. In the solidarity forged of common injury and suffering, whenever one of us was taken for tests or surgery, the rest of us in the ward awaited news that all had gone well. Because of my bandaged chest and the drain in my side, Mum had to do all the talking for me. She offered my fellow spinal patients an optimistic prognosis and a heartfelt thank you for their care and concern.

I was returned to my former bed and delighted to be back in by-now-familiar surroundings among my new friends. I rested my gaze on the little patch of ceiling directly above me—my only view for so many weeks—and found it somehow comforting. Surgeons had pronounced their delicate and dangerous operation to repair my shattered spine a success, so I could begin the recovery process in earnest.

The ritual of blowing on the inspirometer and forced coughing continued for some time. Although the drain in my side was uncomfortable, I dreaded having it removed. I was aware that there could be tissue adhesions, and to make matters worse, the drain was taped firmly to my skin. When the nurse finally came to remove it, my fears were confirmed.

First, the bandage had to be removed in order to extract the drain. I felt the tube moving inside me as they wriggled it free. I was surprised when I saw how long and thick it was, which explained the discomfort. The open wound left by the drain was newly bandaged so it could heal on its own.

By now it had been more than eight weeks since the accident, and I still relied on strong pain medication, no longer administered intravenously but by injection. The nausea that resulted from the drugs combined with my lying flat on my back had thus far made it nearly impossible for me to eat. The mere thought of food repulsed me. My weight, already lean from my athletic conditioning, had plummeted to a dangerous low, worrying everyone and threatening my recovery.

My attending physicians summoned the hospital nutritionist, who explained that every day I spent in bed without moving meant losing one percent of my muscle mass. At this point, I'd already lost around half of it. Preserving and rebuilding my muscle mass meant I could get back to training sooner, so I agreed to a renewed weight-gain effort. My nutritional regimen began with a liquid "meal," advertised as tasting like a chocolate milkshake. I tried my best to force it down; swallowing while lying flat on my back was challenging.

Mum tried to bolster my appetite, as mothers are wont to do. Each day after our visiting time was over, she hurried home to cook my favorites. I tried my best to eat each lovingly prepared meal, but often just the thought or the smell of food made me nauseous. So it was my visitors who often ended up enjoying Mum's home cooking. No matter. Whether or not I ate her meals, Mum resolutely continued to cook them for me without complaint throughout my entire stay in the hospital.

› 7 ‹

With the vertebral repair behind me, I undertook the seemingly interminable vigil of waiting for the bone grafts to heal enough to support my weight. The doctors needed to be absolutely certain of the reliability of that graft, to avoid further damage to my spinal cord. Until then, I would be relegated to forced immobility—a prospect both insufferable and ironic for someone whose life before the accident revolved around movement and sports. I'd have to remain flat on my back, with restricted neck movement, in a ward shared with five other spinal cord injury (SCI) patients for at least the next eight weeks.

Each of us in the spinal ward was well accustomed to the hospital's routine; we could even tell time by what the nurses were doing at any point in the day. Between being a prisoner to my injuries and adapting to the hospital's rigid system, I'd completely lost my independence. I longed to be able to do something, anything, in my own good time and with some modicum of privacy.

Each day started around five thirty, when we were awakened whether we liked it or not. Next came the morning wash, which meant a sponge bath from a nurse because of our bedridden conditions. Not only did each patient have to be bathed and then turned but also his or her linens had to be changed as well. It took two stout male orderlies to shift each patient, along with two nurses attending to the washings and linens.

My post-operative needs were unique: one nurse steadied my head while two men stabilized my back and rolled me onto my side and the remaining nurse washed my back and the more inaccessible parts of my body. While the men kept me on my side, the wash-nurse would somehow slip the sheet from under me and replace it with a fresh one. All of this was orchestrated with the finesse and precision that was the medical equivalent of a car-racing pit crew.

Ever social, I spurred conversation with my attendants to find out what was going on outside the ward—and to deflect attention from the discomfort of this work for all of us. With the six of us chatting, bathing evolved into a more social and less awkward event, dispelling the embarrassment and indignities I'd have otherwise suffered.

The nursing team made its rounds in the ward, repeating this process with each patient before coming around once more to bathe the remaining parts of our bodies. While a nurse sponged my legs and arms, I usually washed my face with my good arm, my left one. Given all that was involved and the imperative to keep SCI patients absolutely stable, bathing was a tedious and time-consuming procedure.

Bath time over, it was then time for breakfast, which came about seven thirty in the morning. A nurse spoon-fed me because I wasn't yet able to feed myself. I still hadn't regained my appetite, so breakfast meant forcing down a few bites of soggy toast and washing it down with tea. My failure to gain weight continued to be a concern, but I was still repulsed by the thought of food and found it difficult to swallow while flat on my back.

Breakfast done, the nurses brushed our teeth, combed our hair, and looked after any other hygienic needs. Despite the tedium and clinical nature of these chores, our morning ritual was extremely important for our well-being. Cleanliness helps a spinal patient feel more human.

The physiotherapists arrived after breakfast. Their job was to administer "passive movements" to keep the joints mobile and to strengthen the wasted muscles of paralyzed limbs. They put us through a series of rigorous and painful stretches, the discomfort a result of our muscles and ligaments having contracted while we were bedridden and immobilized.

I enjoyed this tactile stimulation and so embraced the discomfort that came with it. As I had lost the ability even to touch my own body, it was soothing to be massaged by someone else. That physical connection with a caregiver offered welcome healing for both the body and the mind.

In addition to the physiotherapy, Mum arrived each day, without exception, either before breakfast or while I was being washed. She'd try to ease the staff burden by looking after me as much as she could. Mum sat and chatted, brushed my hair, read to me, and massaged my feet. She was tireless and unwavering in her attentiveness, and it did wonders for my spirit.

Sandwiched in all this routine was the twice-daily need to administer medication. I made it a point to find out what each pill was for. As part of these medication rounds, nurses would attend to each patient's remaining needs, from refilling intravenous solutions and replenishing the antibiotics in them, to emptying catheter bags and checking for infections. Infection—especially of the urinary tract, the dreaded UTI—was common among SCI patients. Once even suspected, UTIs demanded a course of antibiotics and drinking water until we felt we would burst.

Before we knew it, it was time for lunch, followed by more physiotherapy, additional rotation to prevent bedsores, and another round of medication. Dinner was served at four-thirty. How anyone could fathom having dinner at such an hour was beyond me at first, but that was the rule and we all got used to it.

Interspersed in this routine was a constant parade of doctors. The hospital spinal specialist and a medical resident checked on me daily, while my surgeons came at least twice a week. Often as not, they arrived with a group of medical students, who gathered at the foot of my bed and talked about my "case" as if I weren't there. With my knowledge of anatomy and physiology, I thought they should have included me in the discussion, and it annoyed me to be treated like an inanimate subject of their training.

"Here we have a young female, previously an athlete, involved in a major bicycle accident," the doctor might say, giving a summary of my injuries before asking what his subordinates might do in a situation like mine. The fledgling doctors would stand about sheepishly, tongue-tied, and perhaps a little intimidated by the authoritative surgeon. All the while, I was supposed to lie there like a dummy as they discussed my predicament and injuries. I was never one for patience. Often I would find the suspense unbearable and give them a bit of help, blurting out the answers when they took too long. They'd all look aghast at my cheekiness, but I got a real kick out of shaking everything up a bit.

Despite the collective pall of so many tragic injuries, there were positive things about life in the spinal ward: the helpful staff, the faithful visitors, and the companionship of the other patients. But for all these good points, there were many more depressing ones. Chief among them was the loss of identity. After a while, an SCI patient begins to feel like a number in the system and that the whole purpose of the day is to make sure you are turned, washed, fed, and medicated.

Then there were the "unmentionable" aspects of my confinement, which heaped humiliation on top of the other challenges. Because my body had no way of emptying itself of the waste that accumulated in the bowels, this had to be done manually by the nursing staff. In the early days of my hospital stay, I was too sick and in too much pain to fret over this, but as the weeks progressed, it became the single part of my care that I dreaded most.

Since the only partition between beds was the "privacy" curtain, if someone was having their bowels attended to or catheters changed, it was readily apparent to the other five patients sharing the room. Most of the nurses did their utmost to make the process as quick as possible, knowing how embarrassing it must be, but there was the occasional one who was devoid of compassion or sensitivity. These nurses would fail to fully close my curtain, apparently not caring that anyone walking past could plainly see what was happening. Or they would blithely carry on a conversation with another attendant while they worked on me. After such nurses finished with me and moved on to the next patient, I would shed a few quiet tears, feeling stripped of my last shred of dignity by this procedure. Fortunately, such inconsiderate nurses were few.

I was determined to maintain a bit of "self" by asserting my individuality wherever possible. I started by dispensing with the standard-issue white gown. My accomplice in this was a special orderly, Darryl, whom I used to call "Uncle." I first encountered Darryl when I was admitted to intensive care. Through the haze of meds, one thing I was aware of was that my mouth was maddeningly dry. Darryl supplied me with ice cubes to suck on. What blessed relief that was! I'm told of those days that in my delirium I would sometimes cry out in the night, "Uncle Darryl, Uncle Darryl! More ice cubes!"

When I was moved to the acute spinal ward and finally cognizant, Darryl made it a point to formally introduce himself. I found him to be a teddy bear of a man. His large stature belied his gentle voice and demeanor. His caring, light-hearted manner made him an instant favorite of mine.

To my enduring delight, Uncle Darryl always wore one of the patient gowns from the children's ward, which were adorned with cartoon animals. When I told him how much I liked his outfit, he offered to get me one. These playful gowns replaced the cheerless ones I'd been provided. It was my way of reminding both my caregivers and myself that I was a person, not an anonymous patient, and that hope and humor are important in healing.

Uncle Darryl often visited me on his days off, even on holidays. Equally considerate of my family, he brought in a television set for Mum and Dad to use when they stayed in the nurses' quarters on weekends. He'd also use his personal time to sit on the grass outside with Dad and talk, which both men enjoyed. Uncle Darryl became a good friend to all of us, and I loved him for his tenderness and compassion.

In between the attention from staff and visitors, television provided some comfort and companionship. The patients all watched the same programs so we could discuss anything we'd seen. Interested more in the distraction than the value of the programming, we weren't discriminating in our choices: miniseries, news, sports, or rubbish, it was all the same to us. To my delight, the World Cup and Commonwealth Games were on during my stay, and I followed them intently.

Mum discovered a phone connection next to my bed, and the nursing staff allowed me to bring in my own receiver. Making calls was a great boon that helped to lessen my sense of isolation. That phone became my lifeline to the world outside Prince Henry. I would place calls mainly at night, even ringing Mum and Dad to be sure they had made it home. Such were the small pleasures of confinement to the spinal ward.

When our visitors and families departed at the end of each day, there came a new challenge—the loneliness of the night. As staffing wound down for the day to a skeleton night crew, I felt a terrible sense of isolation at being left alone in the ward. This intensified as the night wore on, and I would often cry myself to sleep, wishing I could close my eyes and wake up back in my own bedroom and former life.

One evening before bedtime, the nurse on duty, Wayne, had an idea both to relieve the boredom and lighten the atmosphere. He started to join drinking straws together into a long chain and gave each of us straws to thread together as well. He then proceeded to drape the chain of straws in a continuous line over the curtain railing between each bed. He made sure that the straws hung down over each patient so that we could touch them. The whole thing got crazier by the moment.

"Since we are confined in this place together, I think it is only right that we have a way to express our closeness, that we are bonded to each other," he said. We were unsure where he was headed but also intrigued.

"When I say go, I want you to reach up and grab the straws above your head. Everyone ready? Go!"

We did as we were told and reached up for the straws.

"Okay, now we're all connected!" announced Wayne.

As we began to laugh, the simple truth behind his words struck me. Despite our differences, at that moment, a common thread did join us. Our lives had been irrevocably altered by a panoply of life-shattering injuries, yet we all shared the same challenges, fears, and indignities, as well as the hope for a full and rewarding life once we left the spinal ward. As playful an exercise as it was, I resolved always to remember the truth in Wayne's powerful metaphor of connected straws. I had no way to know then that, years later, I'd have the opportunity to share this moving experience with the world.

Things progressed in my recovery until one night, while watching television, I was seized by stabbing sensations in my chest. At first I tried to ignore them, but when they intensified, I called out to the nurse on duty, who happened to be Wayne. He took a look at me, and I could see the concern on his face. He immediately called the night resident.

To my dismay, I quickly learned about my serious symptoms: I was exhibiting the classic first signs of a pulmonary embolism, or a blood clot in the lungs. This was a major threat for any spinal patient—I'd later hear of the recent deaths from pulmonary embolisms in the acute ward—so the staff was always on the lookout for such a development. The patients most at risk were those with multiple fractures—like me. Any hint of the possibility of embolism signaled an all-out emergency.

The on-call doctor ordered an IV heparin drip to thin my blood and stave off the immediate threat for the night. Showing a lack of both skill and concern, he made multiple clumsy attempts before locating a suitable vein. Daylight brought another doctor to my side, this time a woman who needed still more blood for testing. Taking one look at my pincushion arm, she announced that there was no way she could get any blood from it. Apparently, the first doctor had made such a mess of my veins that there was nowhere left to try. Since my right arm and body were still in plaster, the only other option was my foot.

Soon after, another doctor came to my bedside. He told me I'd soon be transported nearby to Prince of Wales Hospital for some special tests. Though alarmed by the turn of events, I was at the same time excited by the prospect of an outing—it seemed anything was better than the dull routine of the spinal ward.

Riding in the transfer ambulance, I imagined what it must have been like the day of my accident, which I had no recollection of whatsoever. Owing to my neck brace, I couldn't move my head, so I asked the paramedic sitting with me to describe the scenery as we drove. He graciously did so, offering a running account of the streets and suburbs through which we passed. It was a delight to be so engaged in the world outside of Prince Henry Hospital, and it made me realize how much in my life I had previously taken for granted.

Upon arrival at Prince of Wales, I was wheeled to the X-ray department for a radioisotope lung scan. Through a tube in my mouth, I inhaled a gas that allowed doctors to check air circulation in all sections of my lungs. Another radioactive compound was injected into the IV drip in my arm to follow the blood flow and ensure that circulation to the lungs was unimpeded.

After what seemed an eternity, I was relieved to be given the "all clear" by the doctors. I felt a little nauseous after the tests, but they assured me that would pass. Nausea and my chest pain notwithstanding, I had been out for the day, and I enjoyed the adventure.

Before I was returned to Prince Henry though, Mum had arrived at the spinal ward for her usual visit. She was unaware of what had transpired during the night and found my bed empty. Before she had the chance to ask where I was, she overheard two orderlies talking.

"Where's Janine?" Mum heard one ask.

"It's not good news," the other replied. "She's been rushed to Prince of Wales with suspected pulmonary embolism."

"Oh, well, you win some, you lose some," the first one replied, oblivious to my mum standing within earshot.

Mum was numb as she sat down, his callous words echoing in her mind. She, too, was aware of the danger of embolisms. When she asked about my condition, she was told there was nothing to do but wait. She kept an anxious vigil by my empty bed. Never one to show her concerns, Mum was as cheerful as ever when I was returned to the ward—she never let on about the fear she'd endured the entire time I was at Prince of Wales.

It was only much later that Mum told me about it, and I got an inkling of her dread when she overheard "suspected pulmonary embolism" from the staff. The story made me appreciate the anguish and fear that Mum, Dad, and my family experienced at so many junctures of my recovery. I cannot imagine how much they suffered after my accident and during the long recovery. During that time, I was aware only of their unwavering attentiveness, encouragement, and love.

> 8 <

As the bone graft in my back began to fuse and the pain began to subside, the morphine injections were replaced by pethidine, which carried a lower risk of addiction. Despite my doctors' reassurance that it would pass, I had become reliant on strong medication. Not only did morphine ameliorate the pain, but the dreamlike state it created offered me relief from the boredom of lying on my back immobilized. Now, with only this less powerful medication to assuage my discomfort, I had to find some other ways to distract myself from the tedium and the pain.

Roughly two months after my accident, the plaster cast on my right arm was removed. The plaster had reached from my fingertips to below my shoulder, so once we removed it, my arm and wrist were frozen in the form of the cast. Because of the fibrous scar tissue that had developed, I faced two weeks of therapy to dislodge the adhesions and regain full use of my arm. It was time for me to begin working with the physiotherapists to get some mobility back.

The muscles in my arms had atrophied since the accident, so I asked Mum to bring in some of my hand weights to exercise them. Still restricted to a supine position to support my spine, I did strength-building sets while flat on my back. Soon some strength returned, which was encouraging and motivating.

Lower body recovery and mobility were another matter altogether. Without the help of the physiotherapists, I couldn't even lift my legs off the bed. I drew on my athletic will and concentrated all my effort on trying to move them, but to no avail. As the possibility of paraplegia loomed greater with each passing day, I was having a difficult time keeping a positive attitude, try as I did. I wondered if I had heard Dr. Blum correctly when he said the operation was successful. I had taken this to mean I would recover completely and life would return to normal, but numbness and paralysis persisted in my lower body.

Doubts crept into my thoughts. *Shouldn't my legs be a lot stronger—not to mention even the tiniest bit responsive—by now, nearly four weeks post-surgery?* As I learned from my rehabbing arm, my lower body would be weak from all the time I'd spent in bed—that was to be expected. But it was more than just the weakness of my legs that concerned me. Thus far, I had no control over them whatsoever. And what about the numbness and lack of sensation? *Had I only heard what I wanted to hear from Dr. Blum and not the whole truth?*

The doctors continued on their regular rounds, checking to see if I had made any improvement, but their prognoses were vague. Ultimately, one doctor, the rehabilitation specialist, gave me the straight answer I was seeking. A down-to-earth woman, she believed it was wrong to offer a patient false hope. Her approach was to paint the worst possible scenario, thinking that any better outcome would then seem a blessing.

One day when she was at my bedside, I voiced my doubts. Her response started out matter-of-factly: "Janine, it might be a good idea to start thinking about what you will do with yourself when you return home. You will have to make some changes to your life. You won't be able to do the things you did before."

"What do you mean?" I challenged. "I intend to finish my degree, and I have to get back to my ski training."

She drew in a breath and looked at me sympathetically. "Well, that might be a bit unrealistic. Your injuries are permanent, Janine. Once we get you up, we're still not sure if—or how well—you will be able to walk. You may need to use a walking frame or wear braces on your legs to help you."

Braces? Walking frame? I was stunned. I couldn't believe what I was hearing. "But what about my skiing?"

"Janine, it takes time to assess how much normal function you will regain, but you will always have some level of neurological loss. You will have to adjust."

Flat on my back, I could barely see her in the periphery of my vision, but her words rang alarmingly in my head.

"And you may need to rely on the use of a catheter in the future. We will have to wait and see."

With this brief but frank exchange, the dreams and hopes that had sustained me began to evaporate. Everything I had worked for was threatened—my studies, my career, my sports, my body, my future, all of it gone. *Why hadn't someone told me earlier? Had they been stringing me along? How could I believe anyone on my medical team after this?*

My mind spun. I couldn't speak. Dark images and threatening words I'd never before considered flooded my mind: *braces, walking frames, catheters, permanent injuries, never be the same again.* The competitor in me wanted to fight, to prove them all wrong, to reclaim my life. But the reality was that for the time being, I was confined to this bed, immobile and utterly dependent.

In retrospect, I can understand such a clinical approach, because doctors legitimately want to avoid giving a misleading prognosis. But the result of that gut-wrenching talk was that I began to fall apart mentally and emotionally. Until then, I had hidden my doubt and anxiety from my family and friends. I made it my mantra to reassure them how well I was progressing, that soon I'd be out of the hospital and home. Consequently, they too had come to assume that the outlook for full recovery was more likely than it now seemed to be. With the possibility of lifelong impairment, I began to struggle to keep my brave face.

When my visitors left each day, the sadness of watching them go back to their normal routines became too much to bear. My mood sank, and I cried myself to sleep. I ached for my former life. This despondency was something I'd never experienced before—I'd always been an upbeat person who could deal with any setback. I was a fighter and a winner! But the prospect of disability was bigger than any challenge I had experienced before, and now I was in uncharted territory.

So it seemed to me as if my recovery had stalled. There was no indication of when I might be moved from the spinal ward, when I would get out of bed, or when I would go home. An indescribable frustration began to build inside me. *When would this all come to an end?* I'd had enough! I had to get out of bed to see if I could walk. I couldn't wait any longer.

It's difficult to describe the desperate ache of needing to know the future I was facing. For patients in a spinal ward—most of us victims of some horrific accident and facing daunting odds—clinging to the hope of recovery is essential. Once hope is lost, the spirit is crushed, and with it goes our defense against depression. Some of the caregivers knew this and were sensitive; they were the standouts from my time in the spinal ward.

Such was the case with Dominic, the nurse on duty following that terrible conversation. Dom had become my friend and often chatted with me through difficult, sleepless nights. Sensing that something was bothering me, he came around to find me, as I tried to move the stabilizing sandbags on either side of my head.

"Janine, what are you doing?" he asked as he rushed to my bedside.

"I've had enough, Dom! I can't stay still any longer. It's driving me crazy. I have to find out if I can walk. I have to know."

"You can't do that, and you know it. If you try to move, you'll destroy all the work you've done. It'll all be wasted."

"I don't care. I have to move, Dom," I begged.

"Janine, it's hard, I know, but please don't throw everything away now."

He was right. But my frustration boiled over, and in that moment, I lost all reason. "Dom, I don't know what to do. It's as if nothing matters any more." My voice broke, and I started to sob uncontrollably.

"It must be terrible lying there like that, Janine," he offered soothingly. "But you have to hang in there. Let me get some water, and I'll wash your face and arms. That might make you feel a bit better."

Surrender flooded over me. I realized there was nothing I could do but wait and heal. Exhausted from the ordeal, I lay in bed and stared at the ceiling, tears streaming down my cheeks, too despondent to sleep. Dom sat at my bedside most of the night, dabbing my face with a cool, wet cloth and consoling me. His compassion helped me get through my worst night in the acute ward. For that, dear Dom, I will always be grateful.

My depression deepened. I found it nearly impossible to conjure any positive feelings. Realizing the need to help me restore hope, my medical team devised a plan to move me out of the acute spinal ward and into the neighboring ward as soon as possible. Dr. Stephen, the orthopedist who assisted Dr. Blum during my spinal surgery, made it a point to assure me I would be allowed out of bed in a few weeks. The prospect of this lifted my spirits. After four months in the hospital and a bout with depression, I could at last glimpse some light at the end of the tunnel.

Moving to the next ward, called South, proved to be a tremendous boost. One of the first things the doctors did was remove my horrid neck brace. From day one in the hospital, my head had been held rigid against the hard bed. With the brace gone, I was allowed a pillow, a luxury that added to my growing list of small victories.

I was reluctant at first to move my neck, fearful of causing additional damage to my spinal cord. What if the break hadn't fully healed? I had to take things slowly, moving in tiny increments, but much to my relief, all proved fine. With my neck's mobility returning, I could dispense with the mirror over my bed. When the nurse came to take it away, I bid it a silent "so long," wondering who would be using it next and hoping it would be as useful to them as it had been for me.

A common problem for all spinal patients is the constant threat of bedsores from being immobilized for so long. Unrelenting pressure on the skin causes it to break out in blisters, which then ulcerate and become chronic. Because bedsores are both debilitating and slow to heal, prevention is key. Some of my friends had given me the gift of a sheepskin mattress cover for my bed. It helped prevent sores and, along with my pillow and relocation to South, gave me a foothold for pulling myself out of depression.

One of the benefits of being in a busy ward was how readily patients forged friendships with people we would never have had the opportunity to meet under normal circumstances. There we were with our diverse backgrounds, yet for now, we had so much in common. I learned that accidents don't discriminate, and neither does pain and suffering.

Many of my pre-accident friends were full-time student athletes or heavily involved in sports. In the hospital, I found myself learning to appreciate my fellow patients for who they were rather than what they did—and certainly not for their athletic prowess. It was from this new perspective that I came to count a young woman named Maria one of my closest friends among my new circle.

After graduating from high school, Maria took a summer job at a restaurant, planning to start her college studies in art the next year.

Shortly after New Year's Day, Maria's co-workers had invited Maria and her boyfriend to a party. As the festivities wound down, a friend offered to drive everyone to a restaurant in his panel van to continue the party. Ten teens piled in, seven of them in the back, including Maria and her boyfriend. Off they sped in high spirits.

Without warning, the driver's door swung open as they drove around a bend. The driver instinctively leaned over to close it, but in doing so, he lost control of the van, which plunged across the median and into the lane below, where it landed upside down.

Maria was rushed to Prince Henry Hospital with the other survivors. Her boyfriend, a mere sixteen years old, wasn't one of them. Maria lay in a coma for two weeks. She woke on her eighteenth birthday to the news that she would be spending the rest of her life as a quadriplegic.

I heard this story while still in the acute ward and always wondered about Maria. *What did she look like? How was she coping with this tragic turn in her young life?* It wasn't too long before I found out. When I was moved to South, my bed was next to hers.

I learned that this wasn't a coincidence. The patient previously in the bed next to Maria was an elderly woman. The staff thought it would be good for Maria to have someone closer to her own age next to her. While that may have been true for Maria, it was an extraordinary gift for me, too.

Seeing Maria for the first time was heart-wrenching, a stark reminder of how lucky I was to have escaped without even more serious injury. She spent her days strapped in a wheelchair beside her bed, unable to hold herself upright. She could move her head reasonably freely and one arm slightly, but that was all the mobility she was left with. By this point in her recovery, she was able to speak again, although the damage to her vocal cords made it difficult to understand her.

Her wheelchair was straight out of a science fiction movie, festooned with knobs and switches. A lever stretched up in front of her at neck level. She moved this lever with her chin to activate the wheelchair's electric motor and propel herself. She could have done with a few lessons in navigation because she often bumped into things—although she was such a cheeky girl that I often wondered if she sometimes did so on purpose. I was immediately fond of Maria, and our friendship would prove enduring.

As I began to heal and the pain abated, I became concerned with my physical appearance. Before my accident, I hadn't worried about this. I never wore makeup and dressed casually, mainly in track pants, sneakers, and gym shorts.

Lying in a hospital bed, attached to a catheter bottle and various other devices, I found that a sense of self now took on a new importance. I longed to look and feel like a woman. Mum brushed my hair each day and put a ribbon in it—a small gesture I welcomed, but I wanted more.

One of my visitors, Sue, was a beautician, and she offered to give me a facial. She brought in all her products and set about covering my face with a clay mask. In addition to the facial, she gave me a full makeover. I was grateful for the pampering from friends like Sue. Their kindness was an immeasurable contribution to my reconnecting with optimism for recovery. I had lost so much weight—bones protruded from my teddy-bear gown—that the smallest feminine touch helped me to feel human again.

Looking back, one of the greatest intangible benefits from my hospital stay was my deep and abiding appreciation for the friends and family who supported me. Their strength and love rallied me to renew my fight for recovery, reminding me of compelling reasons to heal and get home. They visited at all times of the day—and night—often staying for hours despite the demands in their own lives. Sometimes so many visitors arrived at once that latecomers had to queue up outside and wait their turn to see me.

Despite overwhelming fatigue, it was far more important to me to experience fully the emotional support of those I loved than it was to rest, especially in the early days. My recovery soon became a team effort, with friends and family playing key roles. Their commitment to my healing made me want to get back on my feet for them as much as for myself. I came to appreciate the importance of my relationships, a priceless lesson for which I'll always be grateful.

> 9 <

Dr. Stephen often visited me to monitor my recovery. When I was on the mend both physically and emotionally, he made it a point to recount for me, in detail, the course of the delicate operation—the cornerstone of hope that I'd walk again.

He explained that the two doctors had worked as a team to determine what to do about my spine once they'd determined the extent of the damage. After they'd opened me up—the cut had gone halfway around my trunk—to reach the area of the break, they were confronted with a hopelessly crushed L1 vertebra. This type of fracture, called a comminuted fracture, is typical of high-impact trauma accidents. My surgeon drew a picture for Mum on a piece of paper, which she has to this day, showing the damage as "looking like peanuts that had been stepped on and smashed into thousands of pieces." Because there was nothing left of that vertebra to which they could attach a rod or a plate, the doctors' novel approach was to use my broken ribs to fashion a bone splint.

First, though, they faced the tedious task of removing even the tiniest remaining fragments of my shattered vertebra, painstaking work that demanded the utmost caution to avoid further nerve damage. Next, they extracted one broken rib and inserted it as a prop for the gap left by the vertebra. They packed the space with another piece of rib and larger bone fragments, fusing these with adjoining vertebrae, T12 and L2, to form one large replacement. A second broken rib was used to form a splint on either side of the fusion to strengthen it. The entire procedure lasted more than six hours in the operating room, and it would be at least twelve weeks before we'd know how well the grafts and splints had fused. Such a risky undertaking was pivotal to protecting my spinal cord, and it was the defining step in determining whether I'd be wheelchair-bound for the rest of my life.

To this day, the details of the operation and its daring creativity continue to amaze me.

I could tell from the outset that Dr. Stephen was no run-of-the-mill doctor. A dapper dresser and a bit eccentric, he always wore a colorful bowtie and a smart shirt under his white lab coat. Both he and Dr. Blum were dedicated and hardworking—the best of the best—and I was fortunate to have them on my spinal "repair-and-replace" team.

Dr. Stephen was also an active type, who loved sailing and skiing. With our shared love of the outdoors, we hit it off immediately. He made his rounds at unpredictable hours, sometimes starting his day at dawn, and just as often he wandered the ward late at night and would often find some time to linger for a chat.

"Well, Janine, how are we today?" he might begin. "Have you heard there was a good snowfall this weekend? I think I might head down to the ski resort and investigate."

"Oh, thanks! Rub it in, will you?" I would joke. "When are you going to let me out of here so I can head down there, too?"

Finally, nearly five months after my accident, Dr. Stephen arrived bearing the best news I'd had since I was first admitted: he would be letting me out of bed in a few days! To protect the still-fusing bones in my back, I'd need a fitted plaster body cast before I'd be able to stand on my own. At the time I didn't care—at least I'd finally be mobile!

The body cast fitting required a special type of bed to make the mold, equipment that Prince Henry Hospital didn't have. When the day for fitting the cast arrived, the orderlies came to my bedside, secured me on a metal Jordan frame (an encasing device used to move spinal patients), and once again shuttled me to Prince of Wales Hospital.

Compared to the trip for the suspected pulmonary embolism, this ambulance ride was much more relaxed and enjoyable. Without my neck brace, I was able to look around as we drove. I drank in the scenery during the short commute. Whereas Prince Henry Hospital was a sprawling, scattered collection of rundown buildings, I was pleased to find Prince of Wales Hospital housed in one relatively new, multi-storied building.

I was wheeled into an elevator that rose swiftly to one of the top floors. When the doors slid open, I was wheeled to a smallish room, full of the materials and utensils one might expect to find in an artist's studio, except that it was completely devoid of color. The white sheets on the tables were spattered with white residue (which I concluded was dried-up plaster). A technician wearing, appropriately, a white coat greeted me.

"Hi! You must be Janine. We're going to give you a wonderful new outfit," he offered in a chipper voice. I looked at his hands and noticed that they too were covered in plaster.

"First, we need to get you onto this specially designed bed so that we can work the plaster around you." Using the Jordan frame, the orderlies lifted me onto the center of the "bed"—more like a horizontal crucifix made of steel—with plastic straps across it, similar to those in my Jordan frame.

Before they could build the cast, they had to encase that part of my body in a tube of stretch material—like a body stocking—to prevent the plaster from adhering to my skin. From the look on her face, I could tell that the nurse working with the stocking was stunned to see how thin I was. Because my bones were jutting through my skin, the nurse was forced to improvise and pad me up a bit before the plastering—this way, the hardened cast wouldn't press on my protruding bones and create pressure sores.

The body stocking was tight, but that was nothing compared to the plaster. They ended up wrapping so much of the stuff around me—from my collarbone to my hips—that I had trouble breathing, much less moving. My first thought: *What am I going to do when I regain weight?* I couldn't imagine how I'd attend to day-to-day needs in such a confining and unwieldy suit of plaster armor. But this was a step toward regaining mobility, and that allayed my concerns.

When I returned to Prince Henry, I found that my spinal support bed had been replaced with a model specially designed to tilt from a horizontal position to a vertical one and hold any angle in between. I learned this was part of the preparation for when I'd get out of bed, allowing for the gradual acclimation to being upright again.

I was confined to bed for the next twenty-four hours to allow the plaster to set. I could barely contain my excitement. After months flat on my back, I was thrilled at the prospect of being upright and on my feet. Best of all, this would be a big step toward being discharged.

That night I hardly slept, consumed with anticipation of the next day's physiotherapy. By morning, I was nearly jumping out of my skin with excitement. When the head nurse, Sam, walked into the ward, I almost bowled her over with my eagerness.

"Hey, Sam! Did you hear I'll be getting up today?"

"Yeah, I'd better tell the physical therapists to watch out. It won't be long before you're down at rehab driving *them* crazy." She laughed. It had already become a bit of a joke with the staff that the therapists were dreading the day I started rehabilitation; apparently my reputation for embracing physical challenge had preceded me.

Later that morning, the hospital doctor finally arrived. As he paused, I sensed his discomfort. "Sorry, Janine, I've got some disappointing news," he sighed. "Dr. Stephen just rang to say he wants you to stay in bed for another day. He doesn't think that your plaster is strong enough yet to support your back."

I was crestfallen. Surely he'd misheard Dr. Stephen's directive? I protested in a half-hearted attempt to negotiate, but he was unwavering. He offered his sympathies and left me to myself, my disappointment palpable.

Moments later, Mum walked in, looking as excited as I had been a few minutes earlier. "Hi, sweetheart. All ready for the big day?" she chirped as she put her bag down beside my bed.

"No. I . . . I . . . won't be . . . getting up," I said, as I began to cry. "Doctor's orders are to stay in bed another day to let the plaster set."

Mum knew how much I had been looking forward to getting out of bed, but she tried to put it into perspective. "I know it doesn't seem fair, but Dr. Stephen is only advising what is best for you," she said. "It'll just be one more day, and then you'll be up and forget all about this."

She was right, but I was so emotionally fragile that it didn't take much to push me over the edge. Even this brief delay was a crushing blow, calling into question my trust in the medical team and their seemingly heartless decisions.

Mum left to talk to the nurse. I closed my eyes and tried to drift off to sleep, hoping for refuge from the reality of the hospital and its maddening rules.

I heard a voice at my bedside: "Hey, Nino. How're you doing?"

I opened my eyes to find my friend Tim standing over me.

"Oh. Hi, Tim." I glanced around the room. "Where's Mum?"

"She went down to the shop. She said I should come straight in and see you."

I couldn't hide my emotions. "I'm not feeling that good today. Did Mum tell you the news?"

"Yes, and I'm sorry, Nino. I know you've been looking forward to this for so long." Tim pulled up a chair and sat down beside me.

"Tim, I'm so sad. All I want is to go home and have my life back. Is that so much to ask?" I could sense that everything I had bottled up for so long was about to spill out. I buried my face in my hands and sobbed, unashamed, not bothering to hide my despondency. I was sick of putting on a brave face. After all, there are limits to what anyone—no matter how strong or determined—could endure, and I'd reached mine.

Tim looked at me helplessly, not knowing what to do or say. He took my hand and listened as I continued to pour out my feelings. It was good to let someone in, to share my true concerns, to say things that were so important to me. There was so much on my mind, so many unanswered questions, and so many unknowns.

An additional weight on me of late was a profound sense of guilt, which was tied to an irrational belief that somehow I was responsible for putting my parents through this ordeal. Looking back, I believe this was another symptom of depression.

A final blow that day—and a source of significant torment for me at the time—was a letter I received from the driver of the truck that had struck me:

"Dear Miss Lee," it began (my middle name is Lee—he couldn't even get my name right!). "I am the driver of the car with which your bike collided." (He had struck me from behind. Now how did he see that as *my* having collided with *him*?) "I have looked into the circumstances of the accident and fail to see that I was at any fault . . ." Toward the end of the letter, he added, "But I'm sorry you were hurt and hope you get better soon."

I couldn't shake off the insensitivity and gall in his letter, and his sterile and defensive tone played over and over in my mind. When the young driver ran into me on that beautiful autumn day, he apparently didn't give any consideration to the unalterable consequences the collision had on my life and how it would affect the lives of those who loved me. Nor did he give any thought to my shattered Olympic dreams or my broken body, all irreparably altered at a spot in the road where "my bike had collided with his truck." He never came to see me. He didn't even phone to find out if I had lived or died. Apparently, his only concern was saving his skin in the face of a court judgment on his reckless actions. To think that someone could be so heartless was devastating. His cruel and dispassionate letter haunted me. Even worse, I later learned that his only punishment was a charge of negligent driving, a conviction that cost him a mere eighty-dollar fine.

I've been asked since if I managed to move past my feelings of anger and resentment toward this driver. Naturally, at first I was consumed with anger, and there were seemingly few options for venting it. A social worker at the hospital, Donna, advised me to sit down with pen and paper to write the driver a detailed letter outlining my injuries and how much my life had changed at the hands of his reckless driving. I unabashedly told him how hurt I felt by his lack of contrition and compassion and how he'd affected the lives of my family and friends as well. I wrote his name on an envelope, sealed the letter, and had Mum post it for me. Without an address, I knew it would never be delivered—and I never heard from him again.

› 10 ‹

It was the usual early start for the ward, but not early enough for me. "Good morning, Dom," I said to the nurse on duty the next day. "Today's my big day, isn't it?"

"Yep, you bet. We've come to raise the bed. It'll be a long day for you. Might as well get started." Dom explained that my body would need some time to adjust after being horizontal for so long and that there'd be a progressive inclination of the bed to allow me to acclimate.

"How long will it take until I'm out of bed?"

"It depends on how well you take to being upright, but it usually takes most of the day."

"You're *joking*!" I exclaimed in disbelief. "I was planning to be up before Dad gets here this morning."

"Sorry, Janine, but it'll take a bit longer than that," Dom offered. "If we raised the bed in one go, you could easily faint. Your body has to remember how to function, to pump the blood back to your brain when you're upright."

Dom moved a lever on the side of my bed, and I heard the motor whir and strain to lift me.

"Wow, this is fantastic!" I couldn't help yelling out in my excitement. "Hey, everyone," I shouted to the ward, "I can see you all! I'm getting up today, and it's so great!"

"Good on you, Janine! Well done! Yippee!" There was a chorus of cheers from the other patients at the prospect of one of their own getting up and about, some of whom, like Maria, would never have that chance.

The bed had barely been raised when the motor stopped. My heart sank. "Is this as far as you're going to lift me?" I cried out.

"One step at a time, eh?" Dom explained. "I'll leave it here for an hour or so and see how you go. If you're okay, then I'll raise it a bit more."

An hour? *I guess that's not so bad.* Thus solaced, I resolved to enjoy the new view. Besides, this was the most I'd seen of the ward for the whole time I'd been there.

Dad arrived for the day's visit. He was happy to see the progress I was making.

Not one hour, as promised, but a few hours passed. I was feeling good, so I was confident it was time to raise the bed a bit higher. I called out to the nurse who had since replaced Dom.

"Hey, Fran, do you think you could tip me up a little more?" My request was a thinly veiled demand.

"Are you sure you're okay?" she asked.

"I'm fine, really!"

"All right. I'll raise you a bit higher, but promise you'll tell me if you start to get dizzy." She turned the lever a bit more, and the bed groaned as it pushed me closer to vertical.

I felt the blood rushing to my feet and started to get light-headed, but there was no way I was going to let on to the nurse. I was determined to tough it out, to stop at nothing short of getting out of that damned bed.

By lunchtime, I was surprised to find I had an appetite. As I let myself imagine what it would be like to take my meals upright, the thought of food was no longer repulsive. Ever eager to fatten me up, Mum had sent a dish of pasta with Dad, so I tried my hand at eating in my new position. It was both a novelty and an improvement on trying to eat while lying flat on my back, and I savored Mum's home-cooked meal.

As the day unfolded, I was lifted closer and closer to a vertical position. At about forty-five degrees, the staff put a strap around my waist to secure me to the bed. In the afternoon, the nurse raised the lever to the highest setting, and the bed lurched upward until it could go no farther.

"Oh, wow! This is great!" I exclaimed. I couldn't believe how different everything seemed from my new perspective. I drank in as much of the view as possible.

But not long after I had been moved to upright, my feet began to ache. A wooden board along the bottom of the bed gave me something to rest them on, but the pressure on my still-tender feet was too intense. The discomfort concerned me, but I'd already thought of a palliative.

Earlier, Mum had brought some running shoes for me to wear when I was finally allowed up. Now I asked Dad to put them on my feet.

No sooner had Dad put my shoes on than Daven walked in. He knew that this was the big day, but he was unprepared for the scene that greeted him.

"Hey, Dav, look at me!" I shrieked as he approached. "I'm up here."

I looked a sight: wafer thin, bones protruding, wearing my teddy bear gown and running shoes, with a brightly colored ribbon tying my hair into a high ponytail—all while strapped to a bed that had me towering over everyone else. Daven burst out laughing.

"What do you think of my shoes, Dav?" I said, gesturing to my feet. "I thought I might run a few laps once I'm out of bed—so I'm just getting warmed up."

It was late in the afternoon by the time the nurse, Wayne, came on duty to reposition the bed, which would at last get me standing. As the bed was returned to horizontal, I was aware of butterflies in my gut. Wayne briefed me on what to expect. "First, two of us will lift you by the arms to a sitting position," he explained. "We'll leave you there for a while so that you can get used to that. Once you're all right with sitting, we'll raise you to standing, with one of us on either side to support you. Remember: it's been a long time since you've been upright, so if at any point you think you might get sick or faint, make sure you tell us."

The mere thought of moving my body petrified me. What if the plaster didn't hold up? What if they dropped me? I was nervous and guarded, but pushing doubt aside, I steeled myself for the effort as if at the starting line of a race. "Okay, I'm ready. Let's do it!" I announced, putting on my best game face.

Wayne and the other nurse, Alison, held me by the arms, gently moving me from supine to upright. Dad stood back and held vigil in silence. I could sense his concern for my welfare.

"Okay, Janine. Can you slide your legs around so they're hanging over the side of the bed?" Wayne asked.

My attempt to comply was clumsy and ineffective. "I think you'll have to give me a bit of a hand, Wayne. It's difficult to get my legs to move on my own."

Wayne helped me, and suddenly there I was—sitting on my own! It was such a strange and foreign sensation, altogether glorious and bewildering.

"Can you try to sit upright?" Wayne asked.

Now I was confused. "But I *am* sitting straight, aren't I?"

"No, you're leaning back at quite an angle. Try to move forward."

That's when I realized my senses were out of kilter. If the two nurses hadn't been supporting me, I would have fallen backward. When they came to my aid and pulled me to vertical, my confused senses sounded the alarm that I was about to topple forward out of the bed and onto the floor.

"Hold it, guys! That's too far! I'm going to fall on my face!"

"No, it's all right, Janine. You're actually sitting straight now," Wayne chuckled. "I know it feels a little strange, but you'll adjust."

I felt as if I were drunk and about to keel over, woozy and unsteady just sitting there.

"Are you okay, love?" Dad finally spoke up. He couldn't help but notice my disorientation and express his concern.

"Well, it's pretty strange," I answered haltingly, still struggling to get my bearings. The nurses braced me in a sitting position until I felt a bit more at ease.

It was then that I looked down for the first time at what used to be my athlete's legs. They were atrophied, frail, and weak. I wondered how these spindles would ever support me, much less propel me along on a run or on my skis. This only added to my apprehension, though I replaced my doubts with a silent resolve to strengthen my legs once in rehab.

"Well, Janine, are you ready to try to stand up?" Wayne asked.

"I guess so." I swallowed hard, my earlier display of confidence waning. *This is it. Time to dig deep for courage. Finally!*

Each nurse took a firm hold of one arm and deftly lifted me to my feet. I felt disoriented, as if standing on someone else's legs. Even though the nurses were carrying most of my weight, there was a sense of intense pressure pushing up through my feet.

Please don't drop me.

I stood in place, wobbly but determined, my heart racing. I couldn't stop looking down at my feet, with no idea in the least what to do next. Things an able-bodied person knows instinctively—a simple awareness of her legs and how to move them—eluded me, even as I concentrated with all my might.

"How are you, Janine?" one of the nurses inquired. "Would you like to sit down in your wheelchair and rest?"

"No. First let me try a few steps, please." I had to see if I could move my feet—and if, after the risky surgery and interminable recovery, I'd be able to walk again.

"Okay, but let's take it slow. Concentrate on lifting one foot and moving it forward."

I stared at my feet, but for the life of me, I couldn't remember how to move them. It was as if they were no longer part of my body. What for any toddler would have occurred naturally, even if haltingly, was now beyond the ability of a former Olympic hopeful. Despite all my efforts, it was futile—I could not will my foot to respond.

"Wayne, this isn't working. My legs won't move."

"It's okay, Janine. It'll come. It's going to take some time. Try again."

I shut my eyes and tried to visualize how I used to walk. *Right, Janine, let's concentrate. Lift the left leg and move it forward, away from the body. Focus!*

I looked down and saw that I had slid my left foot forward: I had succeeded in willing it to move! Just a few centimeters of forward progress, but it wasn't the distance that mattered now, only that I'd prevailed. I drew a deep breath and, concentrating intently, succeeded in sliding my right foot forward. Two steps! I looked over at Dad and caught him beaming with pride.

Exhausted with the effort and the disorientation of being upright after so long in bed, I collapsed into a wheelchair that Dad had moved behind me for just this purpose. A wave of satisfaction and relief washed over me. Only two steps today, but I'd do even more tomorrow, and more still the day after that.

Sitting in my chair, recovering from the effort, I was just too excited to get back into bed. I was flooded with an unexpected desire to go outside while it was still daylight, to experience, for the first time since my accident, the world outside of the confines of the hospital.

"Wayne, is it all right if Dad wheels me outside to have a look around?" I asked, with the hint of insistence he was by now familiar with. He grudgingly gave his consent and cautioned both Dad and me against overdoing it—adding the caveat to pay close attention to how I was coping.

"Thanks, Wayne. We won't be long," I assured him.

Dad put a blanket over my legs and pushed me out of the ward and into the hallway leading to the exit. I held my breath in anticipation of the fresh air and the sensation of the sun on my face for the first time in months.

It was late afternoon, but the sun was still strong enough to warm my emaciated body. I basked in its soothing glow, closing my eyes and turning my face skyward to absorb the golden rays. It felt deliciously good. I looked around, taking in the details of the hospital grounds. Every sensation was so intense, so real. I wanted to reach out and touch everything around me, as if experiencing the world for the first time.

Two seasons, fall and winter, had passed while I lay inside Prince Henry. There was a hint of change in the air now, with the scents and sounds of early spring, which until this moment, I realized I'd always taken for granted. I drew a slow, deep breath, savoring the fragrance of the acacia in full bloom. The sight of flowers breaking out of bud and the sound of birds chirping in the trees meant that spring would soon arrive in earnest. It was this and a million other priceless little things that I had missed so. I wanted to drink in as much as I could.

It felt as if the whole world had paused while I was recovering but had started up again with my brief respite from the confines of the ward. I asked Dad to push my wheelchair down the walking path leading away from the hospital. As we moved farther along, I had the most breathtaking realization: the hospital was situated in a beautiful location overlooking the Pacific Ocean, and I could now take in the magnificent expanse of the coastline below.

Overwhelmed with emotion at the sight, warm tears streamed down my cheeks as the last five months flashed through my mind. My world had irrevocably changed. *Would it—indeed, could it—ever be the same again?* There was so much to work out, too many questions yet to be answered. But for this moment, while taking in the vast Pacific and reflecting on the significance of its name, those questions could wait.

Tomorrow—and the tomorrows thereafter—would bring more challenges as I would face life outside the spinal ward. I'd find a way to deal with that. Today I had reached an important milestone. I closed my eyes and took a mental snapshot of the moment, as Dad wheeled me back to the ward.

› 11 ‹

The world for spinal patients embarking on the road to recovery revolves around rehabilitation and occupational therapy (OT). Depending on the level of disability, it is important for each of us to learn—or relearn—certain skills, those critical to leading independent lives once out of the hospital environment. Inevitably, this means a new way of being, both physically and emotionally.

Once I was out of bed and mobile, physical therapy became a key part of a daily regimen. I was assigned to the morning shift for physical therapy but negotiated being excused from OT in the afternoon—instead, I used the afternoon for more exercises.

The day after I first got out of bed, I woke early in anticipation of my inaugural physical therapy session in the gym. I couldn't wait to get started. I was determined to get my legs and feet working again as soon as possible.

Going to the gym for rehab meant that I had to be dressed each day, and this was no simple matter as the plaster made every movement difficult. One nurse helped me maneuver into my tracksuit and gym shoes, and a second helped me get out of bed and into my wheelchair. After breakfast, Dr. Stephen stopped by to look at the plaster and say that it was okay to start rehab. He didn't want me to spend too much time upright for the first couple of days, for fear that my back wasn't yet stable enough.

After he left, Bob, an orderly charged with our transport, arrived to collect the group of patients headed to the gym. Some of the regular rehab patients wheeled themselves out and joined me to wait for the group to assemble.

"G'day. You joining us?" one of them asked.

"Yes, what's it like down there?"

"It's not too bad, but they work you pretty hard."

"Yes, that's what they told me inside, and I can't wait!"

"Well, looks like we better get into the cattle truck," this patient said, pointing to a large van.

"That's our transport?" To me, it looked more like a delivery van.

"Sure is. They squeeze us in one by one," he added with a laugh.

By this time, Bob had returned with the last patient. There were nine of us. He opened the back of the van and wheeled the first three in, putting them in a row in front, and then came back for the rest of us.

"Okay, champ," Bob said, when it was my turn. "Ready to go on board?"

"As ready as I'll ever be."

He pushed me up the ramp into the van, arranged the rest of the patients beside and behind me, and shut the doors. We were indeed packed in. I could see now how the moniker "cattle truck" came to stick.

We were driven across the hospital grounds to where the gym was housed, a low and unremarkable building. Its only distinguishing feature was a clinical sign that said, "Rehabilitation." Bob reversed the loading process and staged the group on the walking path. Those who could manage it made their own way inside. He wheeled me up the ramp for my first glimpse of the facility. As with the rest of the hospital, my first thought was that the place could do with a good coat of paint.

Bob pushed my chair through a large set of glass doors and into the gym. "Okay, Janine," he said. "Enjoy your first day. I'll be back in a few hours. Be good."

Once inside, I was impressed by what I saw. This was just what I'd been waiting for—equipment ideal for my training. There were all sorts of machines and contraptions designed to put life back into wasted muscles. Most of the equipment appeared well used and even worn, but as long as it worked, I didn't mind how it looked.

Stephanie, a physical therapist I recognized from the ward, greeted me. "Hi, Janine," she said cheerily. "We've been waiting for you. Ready for some hard work?"

"The harder the better," I said, rising to her challenge.

She showed me around the gym, explaining what each piece of equipment was for. There was a set of parallel horizontal bars along the walls, like those in a ballet studio, except that these were not there to teach people how to dance but how to walk. I watched a few patients working out on them, pulling themselves along as they tried to coax life back into their legs. After the brief tour, it was time for my session.

"Okay, Janine, what we're going to concentrate on today is getting you to stand all by yourself so you can support your own weight." Stephanie positioned my wheelchair between the two bars and took my hands, helping me to an upright position so that the bars were waist high. "Good. Now I want you to grip the bars and hold yourself up."

For the time being, the strength to stay standing had to come solely from my pushing on the bars, but my arms had also grown weak from the many months in bed. I practiced with Stephanie's help until I was able to get from sitting to standing without her assistance, my wheelchair right behind me for when I tired.

While standing—and generally pleased with my progress—I happened to notice a large mirror, placed so the patients could watch themselves walking, as a learning aid. It was the first time since the accident that I had seen myself in full view, and I was dumbstruck by the gaunt figure staring back at me. The clothes I wore hung on me like a sack. My legs were little pegs, weak and thin. My body, once muscular and athletic, had been reduced to a bag of bones. I knew I had lost weight, but to be faced for the first time with the full extent of atrophy was shocking. I stared at the reflection of this strange person who was supposed to be me, and I sagged under the weight of the reality.

"It's a bit of a shock, seeing yourself for the first time, isn't it?" Stephanie offered.

Overcome with dejection, I couldn't even answer.

"Don't worry. Now that you're up, you'll start putting on weight quickly. And the muscle will come back, too, after you've been working out for a while."

At that moment, Mum walked through the door. She had missed seeing me get out of bed the day before—now she was seeing me on my feet for the first time since I'd left home the day of the accident. Not a word was spoken as our gazes met in mutual understanding. I watched as tears welled up in her eyes and rolled down her cheeks. I suspect she had feared she might never see this day. The emotional exchange overwhelmed me, and I began to cry as well because I had often feared the same.

As Mum came closer, her expression warmed into a smile. She leaned over and kissed me on the cheek, whispering, "You look fantastic!"

Engaging Mum at eye level was an extraordinary experience that belied its simplicity. She and Dad, alone and together, had given me more support and love than I could ever have wished for. I couldn't imagine how I'd have managed my recovery without them. Now, facing Mum and standing for the first time in five months, the joy in her eyes told me she felt all her efforts were worthwhile.

"Okay, Janine," said Stephanie, breaking the spell. "Next, I want you to try to move one foot forward while holding on to the bars. I'll walk behind you with the wheelchair so that when you need to sit, it will be right there."

I looked down and concentrated. Calling on all my strength, I slid one of my legs forward a fraction.

"Janine, you're looking at your feet," she admonished. "I want you to try to look up at the mirror when you walk."

I tried again. Willing my feet and legs to respond required all my concentration. Regardless of my effort, my feet just flopped around. I had no control over their movement or placement. I was stymied and disheartened. How could something as simple as a footstep prove so difficult? By then, my legs were rubbery, and my arms ached from holding up my bodyweight. Resigned, I collapsed into my wheelchair.

I later learned that I'd lost the innate ability to perceive the placement or movement in an extremity. For someone who is able-bodied, the mind is always tuned in to where any given part of the body is in relation to the rest of the body, a hardwired ability known as proprioception. That's how we walk without the need to look at or think about our feet. But the damage to my spinal cord interfered with my brain's messages to my legs. I would have to consciously create a new mind-to-extremity pathway to know where to place each foot, one shuffling motion at a time.

Stephanie stayed with me while I practiced my walking most of the morning, until we all stopped for a well-earned tea break.

I took stock of the other patients in the gym. Many were from areas of the hospital other than the spinal unit. I shared the support bars with some of the amputees, who were learning how to walk and balance using crutches. Other patients spent their time doing body exercises on a floor mat or catching a large medicine ball that the physical therapists tossed to them. It was a humbling environment and at times dispiriting, but I resolved to train for my recovery as hard as I had for any competition.

My endurance increased as I spent hours each day practicing my walking and standing and trying to catch the medicine ball without falling over. My wobbliness combined with the cumbersome body cast made staying steady on my feet almost impossible.

But soon my sense of balance began to return, and I required less support from my arms. When I reached that point, the physical therapists added other exercises that proved equally challenging. On one occasion, Stephanie made me stand against a rail to exercise my calf muscles by pushing off the balls of my feet. It should have been easy, but try as I might, I couldn't generate a flicker of movement. *How could I not even stand on my toes?* I tried repeatedly, but nothing happened.

"Why can't I move?" I lamented to Stephanie, and partly to myself.

"We weren't sure if you would be able to do this movement, Janine," she explained. "You've lost a lot of strength, which we can rehabilitate with PT, but you've also suffered a lot of nerve damage, which we can't rebuild. There may be some muscles that never regain their normal function. We'll have to keep working on it to see how much we can get back."

I dismissed outright the idea of never regaining the use of my leg muscles, convinced it was only a matter of more time and harder training. Sure, I had a lot of work ahead of me, but I'd been conditioned as a competitor to demand the most of my mind *and* body. Learning to walk again might be a challenge, but I believed I would not only walk; I would run, ski, and do all the things that I had done before.

With each passing day in rehab, I drove myself to do a little better. Once the van delivered our group to the gym, I tackled each of the planned activities with gusto. I was driven and wouldn't stop until I was exhausted. The only break I took was for a brief mid-morning tea.

From the first day of rehab, I'd been eyeing the facility's exercise bikes. It wasn't long before I experimented and found—to my own and everyone else's surprise and delight—that I could manage to move the pedals around by myself, albeit clumsily. Besides giving me a sense of achievement, stationary cycling added welcomed variety to my rehab. It became my favorite activity.

As the weeks passed, I persisted in pushing myself ever harder, accomplishing with increasing skill each of my exercises in the gym. Most days I squeezed in two rehab sessions, sometimes continuing my practice by walking with Dad in the hall outside the ward. All the while gaining strength, I improved to the point where I could walk with just the support of one person beside me.

My "walk" wasn't the conventional locomotion of each foot following the other. Partial paralysis in my lower extremities made my gait more of a shuffle. Summoning great concentration, I would slowly move my leg to drag that foot forward, then slide the other up to meet it. It was a tedious process, but it worked. Clumsiness aside, I was grateful to move under my own power, to be "walking" against all odds.

With regular practice, I soon built up a strength and endurance that encouraged the physical therapists to up the stakes: they put me to work on a set of dummy stairs outside the gym. Sliding my legs forward was one thing, but commanding them upward was quite another. Once I succeeded in placing a foot on the next riser, there wasn't yet enough strength in my legs to lift my body to join it. I was reminded yet again how much I had taken for granted before this accident. Now even the smallest tasks, formerly done without a second thought, loomed as tremendous obstacles.

Undaunted, I registered small victories as important milestones in my ever-improving physicality. Hoping to wean myself from depending on the physical therapists, for example, I worked out a way to walk on my own by pushing my wheelchair ahead of me, leaning on it for support.

"Hey, Janine, you're meant to *sit* in the chair, you know," the nurses would joke.

However odd it may have appeared, from then on, I was rarely seen sitting in my chair, and everyone became accustomed to seeing me push it around the ward.

Deep in training for competition, Daven brought his "roller skis" to the hospital with him when he visited. Cut-off metal skis fitted with wheels, they were designed for asphalt or similar surfaces and helped him maintain fitness in the off-season by mimicking skiing movement. Daven would "ski" around the parking lot, and I would sit in my wheelchair and watch him, hardly bothering to hide my envy of his fluid and confident strides.

One day, as Daven was roller skiing in the parking lot, he called out to Dad and me: "Hey, Mr. Shep, how about a race?"

With that, Dad took off running, pushing my wheelchair, and it wasn't long before we were fast on Dav's heels. The competition flame still flickered inside me. "Ha! You think you're pretty fast? Well, catch us if you can," I dared, as we overtook him. As we turned the corner, my chair tipped up on one wheel, forcing me to lean the other way to stay upright.

I got caught up in the energy of the race—it was the most fun I'd had in ages. It was obvious that Dad was having a ball, too, but when Mum caught a glimpse through the ward window of what we were doing, she came running out, waving her arms in alarm.

"What do you think you're doing?" she demanded at the top of her lungs. "You stop that right now!"

Dad slowed down and offered his best contrite look, but when I caught his eye, I saw he'd enjoyed it as much as I had.

As we slowed to a walk, I noticed my little car parked in the lot. I had loaned it to Daven to use while I was in the hospital. I asked Dad to wheel me over to it, close enough to peek inside. My gaze was drawn to the back seat, where I saw some of my sporting gear. My heart seemed to stop, and I held my breath. Everything was exactly as I had left it on the day of the accident, as if frozen in time: roller skis, tracksuits, running shoes. I wondered when, if ever, I would be able to use them again. I turned my gaze away and did my best to cover the sinking feeling in the pit of my stomach.

It was getting late, time for Daven to head home. Dad bid him goodbye and returned to the ward, granting me the first opportunity to be alone with Daven since the accident. Limitations imposed by my injuries aside, it had been impossible to have any privacy while bedridden, with only a curtain separating me from other patients and caregivers. Besides, it had taken all of my emotional resources to deal with being confined to the spinal ward.

As a result, my relationship with Daven had suffered during my entire confinement in the hospital.

I would be coming home soon, but even then I'd be starting a long road to recovery and a new way of living. I had no idea what would happen between Daven and me then. Part of me wanted our lives as a couple to pick up where we had left off. But in my heart, I questioned if that would happen—indeed, if it even *could*. So much had changed. How could I ever expect him to understand what I had been through or to envision the future I was now facing? Confined to a wheelchair, attached to a catheter bottle, encased in a plaster cast, I wondered if this young and able-bodied man would still feel the same about me as he had before my accident.

We chatted idly for a bit, and then he embraced me for a kiss goodbye. I closed my eyes and melted into his arms, flooded with the feeling of how much I missed moments of intimacy, of emotional and physical connection. For the last five years of our lives, we had been inseparable. Kissing him now gave me a glimpse of normalcy. I didn't want the moment to end—if only he could scoop me up and take me back to our old lives. Instead, he climbed into my little car and drove out of the hospital gates, taking a piece of my heart—and our history together—with him.

⟩ 12 ⟨

Dr. Stephen's resident physician dropped by one morning to check up on the patients under his mentor's care. Mum and Stephanie were standing at my bedside when they spotted him at the nurses' station. They both paused and stared.

Mum was the first to break the silence, "Wow, Janine, you should see your doctor's resident. He's so handsome!"

Stephanie stole another look at him and then turned to me. "I think I might hang around for a while in case he needs a hand," she said cheekily.

He walked over and introduced himself. "Good morning, Janine. My name is Adrian Cohen. I work with Dr. Stephen."

"Good morning, Dr. Cohen," I replied, returning his air of formality. I could see Mum and Stephanie standing behind him, smiles playing at the corners of their mouths. Mum was right. He was gorgeous! Tall, dark hair, a solid build—this young doctor cut a dashing figure.

"Oh, please call me Adrian," he said, softening. "How is the body cast going?"

"Well, actually it's starting to hurt my back," I said, exchanging a quick glance with Mum. "I think it's pushing against a bone."

"Let me have a look." He pressed various spots on the plaster until I let out a yelp. "Right, then. It seems I've found the spot."

"Yes, and with my rehab and recovery, it's getting increasingly uncomfortable. Can you do anything about it?"

He took a moment to consider the cast a bit more closely.

"What I can do is drill a little hole, like a window, so that the bone doesn't press on the plaster. I'll have a word with the boss, and with his permission, we should be able to do it tomorrow."

"That'd be great. What time will you be here?"

"First thing in the morning," he assured me. "If you have any more trouble before then, get one of the nurses to give me a call, and I'll come up."

What a bonus to my recovery: my own good-looking doctor, on call!

The next morning he returned with the tools and equipment necessary to make adjustments to my cast. Instructing me to hold still, he turned on a drill and began to gingerly cut away the offending plaster.

"Could you take away a little more?" I asked when he stopped, still feeling the discomfort.

"All right. I'll take a bit more off, but that's it. I can't take away too much, Janine, or it could affect the integrity of the cast."

Adrian, or "Ado" as I came to call him, became a regular visitor and welcome distraction from the boredom of the spinal ward. Although neither of us sensed it at the time, he would prove to be a friend and lifelong ally.

My desire to go home intensified as my mobility and strength improved. It seemed there was no longer anything the hospital could offer that I couldn't get at home. After so many months away, I ached with homesickness, longing to spend the night in my own bed and to wake up to the smell of Mum's home-cooked breakfasts.

At the time of my accident, Mum and Dad had been in the process of moving from a rental townhouse to their dream home, on which they'd continued construction while I was in the hospital. Dad brought a video he'd made of the new house during one of his visits—his virtual tour through the then-unfinished house.

"This is where your bedroom will be, and if you walk through the door here, you'll notice we're now standing in the bathroom," he began. I was relieved to learn it was a single-story construction, which would make it a lot easier for me to get around in my wheelchair. He continued his narration, room by room, taking great pride in giving me my first glimpses of our new home.

Watching the video intensified my longing to be back at home with my family. I'd been lobbying for discharge recently, but Dr. Stephen and my rehab doctors were firm about considering only a trial release at first, for just one weekend. If that went smoothly, they promised they'd consider letting me go home for good.

But it wasn't going to be quite so simple as that. I was disheartened to learn that a pivotal consideration in allowing me to go home was that I first needed to learn how to use a catheter without a nurse's aid. The nerves that normally command the bladder to evacuate itself were not yet functioning. Like other aspects of my recovery, I believed it was only a matter of time until they revived. Until then, self-catheterizing was another new and distasteful skill I had to master.

For the extent of my hospital stay thus far, I had used an "indwelling catheter," which drained continuously into a pouch so that I never had to think about emptying my bladder. Now it was time to graduate to an "intermittent catheter," one that had to be inserted each time I felt the need to urinate—a process I immediately disliked because it was humiliating and exhausting.

Here's how my instruction progressed: every few hours, a nurse would come to my bedside with a disposable catheter, a bedpan, and a large mirror. I was then to sit up, with the mirror positioned between my legs. Self-catheterizing meant negotiating the placement of this impossibly small plastic tube into my urethra and threading it all the way into my bladder so that I could void it myself. Learning to do this was demoralizing, often bringing me to tears. Worse still, being awakened every few hours during the night to practice the procedure in a groggy state guaranteed I'd learn to loathe the self-catheter. But I wanted to go home so badly that I forced aside my distaste and tried all the harder to master the technique.

Finally, I was given the go-ahead to schedule my first trial visit home. As the targeted weekend approached, the head nurse, Sam, dropped by my bedside for a no-holds-barred conversation with Mum and me.

"Janine, I want to warn you that things will be pretty hard during your first time away from Prince Henry."

"What do you mean?" I couldn't fathom how being home again would be anything but sheer delight.

"We find that patients returning to their homes have trouble adjusting to the change of routine. In the hospital, they're treated like everyone else and on a set schedule. But at home, they're the odd ones out, having to do things on their own and manage their time. That can be disorienting, even upsetting. A lot of our patients feel sheltered here and put off going home as long as possible."

"Not me, Sam. I can't wait."

"That's fine, and I wish you the best. But nonetheless, you should prepare yourself for a bit of a shock."

I listened to Nurse Sam but found it hard to imagine how anyone could want to stay in the hospital any longer than necessary. I made a mental note of her counsel but didn't allow it to dampen my enthusiasm. I was ready to be back in my own room, with my personal belongings, and to start the process of picking up where I had so suddenly left off. I had a lot of time to make up.

Finally, all of the necessary arrangements were in place. I was to leave the hospital on Friday, after the doctors' morning rounds, and return that Sunday afternoon. The doctors and nurses had briefed Mum and Dad on what to expect and had given us a list of what to take: my wheelchair, along with the essential clothes, medications, and catheters. I made a point to say goodbye to my friends in the ward. Though I would be home for only two days, I'd already begun the mental preparations for separating for good from the sanctuary of the hospital.

I wheeled myself outside to meet Dad, as he packed my bags into the car. I wanted to sit in the front, but with my plaster body cast, the passenger seat proved too tight a fit. Instead, Dad helped me to my feet, lifted me in his arms, and placed me on the back seat. I struggled at first to find a comfortable position. With the plaster cast extending the entire length of my trunk, sitting wasn't a simple matter. I wiggled around until I got myself settled and waved goodbye to Sam and the other nurses.

As we drove away, my excitement gave way to a feeling of gnawing apprehension. It dawned on me that for the first time since my accident I was about to encounter the world beyond the protective hospital environment. With my new and challenging disabilities, the prospect of being home began to feel unnerving. I thought about Sam's admonition and felt the first pangs of fear. *What if I wasn't ready to go home, after all?*

I shrugged off my doubts, as I took in the unfamiliar surroundings on the way to our new home. I had never been through this part of Sydney before, so Dad offered a running commentary along the way to help me get oriented and to distract me from the discomforts of travel.

It was peak afternoon traffic hour in the bustling city, and I noticed the streets were full of people hurrying home from work. Just like me before my accident, they were wrapped up in their own cares—thoughts of spinal cord injuries or paralysis were likely the furthest things from their minds. Did any of them even know a whole other world exists inside the walls of Prince Henry Hospital, especially within the confines of its acute spinal ward? I envied the ease of their movement. It looked so simple, the way they lifted their feet without having to think about it. I remembered when I could move with the grace and endurance of an Olympic athlete—flying effortlessly on multi-hour runs. I was certain they'd never considered how difficult life could be after a spinal cord injury. Regardless of what the future held for me, I vowed never again to take such gifts for granted.

My attention returned to inside the car where my physical limitations grew increasingly uncomfortable. Even this relatively short commute was beginning to push the limits of my stamina. I had never before noticed how rough the city roads were. Each bump seemed to go right to my sensitive spine. Tired and uncomfortable, I told Dad I needed a break.

He stopped at a park and helped me out so that I could stretch my legs. The spot we'd picked was on the harbor, looking back over the city. I watched drivers zoom past on their way to start their weekends. The water was dotted with pleasure craft out for an evening sail. I glanced at my watch: dinnertime at the hospital. I knew what everyone would be doing and felt the first pangs of separation, as Dad loaded me back into the car for the last leg of our journey.

"Well, this is it!" Dad announced, as we pulled into the driveway.

"Oh, it's beautiful. Just like in the video," I sighed.

No sooner had Dad stopped the engine than Mum rushed out to meet us. "Welcome home!" she exclaimed and gave me a kiss. "How was the trip?"

"Well, it was a bit tiring," I admitted. "I didn't realize it was such a long way!"

"Let's get you inside. We'll get you settled first, then have dinner." Dad helped me wriggle out of the seat, slipped his arm around my waist, and supported me as I made my way to the front door. Though weary, I was far too excited to miss out on the opportunity of having a look around. Even though I had yet to set foot in this house, I was with my family—I was at home.

"Can I see my bedroom first?" I wanted to see my belongings, all the special, personal things I had so missed while I'd been in the hospital.

"Okay. First stop: Janine's bedroom," Dad said, in fine tour-guide fashion, pushing my wheelchair up the hallway.

I was astounded when I saw my new room. Mum had arranged all of my things just as I would have. There was a full-length mirror on the wall. I got a lump in my throat when I saw myself in it, sitting in a wheelchair. Throughout my childhood, I had always delighted in being alone in my room. I knew I would cherish having my private space once again. *I belong here, and I never want to go back to the hospital again.*

Behind me was the cabinet where Mum displayed all my trophies. Mum opened the wardrobe, and I looked at the clothes she'd hung up for me. I picked up a neatly folded tracksuit with the words "Australian Ski Team" embroidered on the front. With Mum's help, I put it on and looked at myself in the mirror. My heart sank when I remembered I'd missed the entire winter training season—and who knew when I might ski again.

Dad wheeled me into the kitchen, where my senses were overwhelmed with the rich sight and smell of Mum's homecoming dinner: baked chicken with my favorite vegetables. Kim and Kelley no longer lived at home, so it was just the three of us. After Dad positioned my wheelchair at the table, we gathered for our first dinner as a family in nearly half a year.

Our family didn't usually say grace, but on this special occasion, Dad asked us to join hands for a blessing. I stole a glance his way and could see the tears well up and roll down his cheeks. He squeezed my hand as he offered his thanks for having his baby girl home from the hospital. On my other side, Mum did likewise. Witnessing this unabashed show of emotion, it was evident the tremendous toll my accident had taken on my parents. I could sense the heartbreak, fear, and sadness they'd endured over the past months and how my struggle to recover had demanded so much of their energy. Saying grace took on a new meaning and importance for us all. I had never been so grateful to be home, nor had I ever felt closer to my parents.

Before Mum helped me into bed that night, she demonstrated the intercom system they installed, which linked my bedroom to the rest of the house. Mum assured me that she and Dad would hear me call if I wanted something or had any problems, and that I shouldn't hesitate to page them. She kissed me goodnight and headed off to bed.

Alone in my room, I was struck by the heavy silence that enveloped me. I had anticipated this moment of privacy and peace in my own bed, but now my room seemed too quiet and dark. Accustomed to sleeping in a noisy ward with so many other people and around-the-clock activity, I was overwhelmed now by loneliness tinged with fear. I closed my eyes and tried to force sleep, but my mind started racing.

My thoughts flashed back to the last time I'd slept in my own bed, the night before the accident. My friend Chris had arrived that afternoon, and we had gone on a training run together. In the evening, we watched television and talked late into the night, discussing our plans for the ski season. We reminisced about our training and the traveling we'd done together on the world ski-racing circuit. We talked of our love of Yellowstone National Park—a snow-covered fairyland where ski tracks wound through the forests—and of a bitterly cold day in Minnesota when, oblivious to the threat of the weather and thinking only of the race, I'd given myself a bad case of frostbite.

My reverie was shattered by a sinking realization: as I lay awake, encased head to toe in a body cast, I knew I wouldn't be traveling, training, or racing with the Australian National Ski Team this season. I tried to assure myself that with hard work and determination I could be back in top shape for the following year. I closed my eyes and drifted off to fitful sleep.

I spent most of the weekend in a daybed in the lounge room, which Mum had set up for me. My body cast was so heavy and confining that

I couldn't sit for very long. Another, more nagging discomfort—no surprise—was my catheter. It took multiple attempts to get it right. I despaired at the prospect of venturing outside the house until I could manage going to the bathroom without so much effort and frustration, not to mention the still-required mirror.

Even with such low levels of activity, I tired easily and needed to spend much of the day sleeping. It wasn't just the physical fatigue; the emotional stress of coping with my limitations drained me as well. Discomfort and exhaustion notwithstanding, my first weekend at home passed all too quickly. I wanted to stay longer and persuaded Mum to phone the hospital on Sunday to negotiate one more night in my own bed. The doctors acquiesced, and my reprieve was extended to Monday.

Once back at Prince Henry, I uneasily slipped back into the routine of the spinal ward. The lack of comfort and privacy was now all too evident compared with my bedroom. When at last the week drew to an end, I again bid my friends farewell and exited the hospital gates, tremendously relieved for another trial weekend at home.

Now that I was familiar with the new house, I settled in more quickly than I had on the first visit. I was getting used to sleeping on my own, the silence no longer such a challenge. That second weekend stay also seemed to fly by, and another phone call to the hospital (which I imagine they'd come to expect by this time) granted me an extension to Monday morning.

That Monday at Prince Henry, though, proved to be a most auspicious day. When my doctors heard how well I was managing at home, they agreed that I could leave again on the following weekend—for good! Arrangements would be made to continue my rehab at a hospital closer to home, so there'd be no need to return to Prince Henry.

I could hardly believe what they were saying. After almost six months in the hospital, enduring a slow recovery and too many tears to count, I was at last being discharged. I could begin my new life in earnest.

I spent the final evening of my time in the hospital talking with Maria. She was also scheduled for discharge, except that her transfer would be to a nursing home for long-term quadriplegic care. I gave her my phone number and address, promising to visit as soon as I was able. Maria was a paragon of optimism and would prove to remain so for the rest of her life. Her unwavering good cheer in the face of her devastating injuries was a valuable reminder to me to keep a positive attitude as I traveled my own long and uncertain road of recovery.

The morning of my discharge from Prince Henry couldn't come soon enough. Mum arrived early and packed up my belongings and all the medications I'd need. Just as I was about to leave, Ado came to say goodbye. He asked if he could ring me when I got settled at home. He said he had some tickets for a show in a few weeks and was hoping I might join him.

I was flattered by the invitation, not to mention a bit surprised. Gaunt, encased in a body cast, unable to walk, and attached to a cathe-ter bottle, I hardly cut the figure of an appropriate date for a handsome and eligible doctor. With my self-esteem at such a low, being asked out by such a catch as Ado did wonders for my confidence. But I politely declined his offer, explaining that I had a boyfriend and felt the outing would be inappropriate.

I had grown fond of Ado. I enjoyed his company and our conver-sations, so I couldn't tell him that his invitation had little to do with Daven. Really it was more that I was too emotionally fragile to go on a date. Undeterred by my refusal, Ado insisted on taking my number and promised to call me.

As Dad lifted me into the car, one of the nurses came running toward me, pushing my wheelchair. "Janine!" she shouted. "Haven't you forgotten something?"

"Actually . . . no," I stated flatly. "I left it intentionally. I won't have any need for it."

She gave me a puzzled look. "But then how will you get around?"

"Don't worry," I assured her. "I'll be fine without it."

I watched the dilapidated buildings of Prince Henry Hospital vanish behind me as we drove through the hospital gates for the last time. Leaving my wheelchair behind meant giving up some inde-pendence, but no matter my prognosis, I resolved to get around the house—and back to a normal life—on my own feet.

› 13 ‹

Because my spinal cord had been partially severed as well as crushed, certain key nerves were damaged beyond repair. The resulting loss of both neurological function in my muscles and sensation in the lower half of my body had rendered me—in medical parlance—a partial paraplegic. On the one hand, I was informed that the spinal cord damage was permanent, but on a more hopeful note, the doctors also said it was possible for other nerves to take over for the damaged ones (called "neuroplasticity"). Uncertain about the prognosis, they couldn't yet predict the extent of expected recovery. They were careful not to get my hopes up. But on one point they were clear: whatever recovery I achieved within the next two years would be the ultimate extent of nerve function and improvement in mobility. Given this sliver of hope, I was convinced that with enough hard work, I could retrain my nerves and muscles to function as they had before.

With the two-year clock ticking, it was important I get to work on my recovery straightaway. I had already suffered extensive muscle atrophy in my lower body: my feet had changed shape, and my toes were clawed—something common with spinal cord injuries. These deformities made it nearly impossible to wear shoes, to say nothing of trying to stand. To make matters worse, I had also lost strength and function in my buttocks and hamstring muscles. In short, it would be challenging just to stay upright, much less to try to walk without aid. Facing these limitations, I began the next phase of my rehabilitation at a new and more modern rehab facility, Westmead, the hospital where my life flight was destined before it was diverted.

My workout routine there was similar to the one at Prince Henry. I spent the first part of the morning practicing walking with the parallel bars and the fake stairs and then half an hour on an exercise bike. Along the way, the physical therapists introduced a few other aids, such as the balance board, an oval piece of wood with a ball underneath. The object was to stand on it while holding onto the bars and to balance as the board wobbled underneath me. Though it required increased concentration, the balance board did wonders for strengthening my feet and ankles. I also worked with resistance-training equipment designed for rehabilitating injury-damaged muscles. This helped me regain the strength I'd need in my thighs to compensate for my atrophied and unresponsive lower legs.

It wasn't long before sessions at Westmead grew tedious, and I became bored with the routine. Not only wasn't I being adequately challenged, but I also grew concerned I wouldn't make the progress I desired within that two-year window of opportunity. It helped when I learned there was a pool at the hospital. I decided to incorporate swimming into my rehab program as soon as I was permitted to do so.

Still in my plaster body cast, I asked the physical therapists if we could have a look at the pool. I was crestfallen when I saw it was only a small hydrotherapy pool, used mostly by older people holding on to the edge and doing palliative exercises. The soothing heated water allowed patients to perform exercises in a weightless environment, which placed much less demand on the body. I'm sure it met its purpose for certain applications, but it wasn't what I'd hoped for. I wouldn't be swimming laps there.

With any pool out of my reach for the time being, my plodding progress became a greater source of frustration for me. *Why weren't my legs getting stronger? When would the feeling return to my lower extremities?* I longed to get back to skiing and competitive athletic training, but I still struggled to stand, much less walk. My dreams of returning to ski racing began to fade, and along with them, my optimism once again began to flag.

Adding to these mental and emotional threats were the long days at home. Without a wheelchair, I remained immobile unless aided. Once I seemed settled to them, my friends visited less often and got on with their own lives, and I found myself increasingly isolated. To all appearances, I was coping with my indoctrination to disability, but secretly I had begun again to experience symptoms of depression, which until then I had busied myself enough to stave off.

And still I struggled to accept my damaged body and the limitations my injuries imposed. I resented the idea of being physically disabled, and I hated having to rely on medications, catheters, walking aids, and other paraphernalia for day-to-day living.

But by far it was the hidden and "unmentionable" aspects of spinal cord injury—bladder and bowel dysfunction—that caused me the greatest emotional distress. My spinal cord damage left me with significant loss below the lumbar level. Now it appeared I was facing a future in which my body required painstaking attention to each limb, function, and activity. It was a heart-wrenching fall from the grace of my days as Australia's top female skier—indeed, as one of the top ski racers in the world.

Adding to my despair were the times my athlete-friends dropped in to visit, often riding their bikes on their way back from a training session. They meant well, but the updates on their lives and training only deepened my sense of loss. I steeled myself to smile and engage in the pleasantries of conversation, all the while aching with a profound longing to train with them once again. I yearned to put on my athletic shoes and head out for a simple run, but now I feared I might never be able to do that again.

As I fought the tedium of rehab and stalled recovery, it didn't help that medical follow-ups demanded I talk about my injuries to doctors and other medical staff, many of whom seemed cold and businesslike. Their medical briefings served to focus my attention on how much my life had changed and on how different I was from the able-bodied around me. I had hoped for a reprieve from such clinical discussions once I was discharged, but each checkup meant revisiting things I longed to put behind me.

One particular visit to a clinic presented me with the most embarrassing and humiliating discussion yet. I was seated in the office of an insensitive doctor when I heard the pronouncement that would haunt me for years to come:

"Janine, you seem to be doing well with your recovery," he began, glibly. "So, I think this would be as good a time as any to discuss the impact your injury will have on future sexual function."

"Um . . . I really don't feel comfortable talking about that with a total stranger," I stammered, caught off-guard. I was a twenty-four-year-old woman and he was a fifty-something-year-old man, and this wasn't a subject I felt was appropriate to discuss with him.

"Yes, well I can understand that, but most patients find it easier this way," he countered, undeterred. "Let's face it, Janine, a spinal cord injury affects every part of your life, so it's something we do need to talk about."

"Well, isn't there a lady doctor I can speak to?"

"Unfortunately, our female specialist is overseas, so that leaves me, I'm afraid." Clearly, he would not be swayed from his mission. "Now, Janine, I am not suggesting that you won't have a sex life," he began, condescendingly. "Sexual gratification can take many forms, emotional as well as physical. But with your level of spinal cord injury . . . well, it will be unlikely that you will be able to have the . . . er . . . the 'Big O' again."

I shifted in my chair. Oblivious to the discomfort my body language conveyed, he blithely continued, "But of course there are many normal, healthy women who have never experienced one, and it hasn't been the end of the world for them. I'm aware this is a delicate discussion, Janine. Sooner or later, one way or another, this is an issue that must be faced. How you handle it is up to you."

Humiliated and embarrassed, I fought back my tears, determined at all costs not to cry in front of him. I refused to give him the pleasure. I used small talk instead to deflect the attention from such a personal affront, but inside I was outraged. *How could anyone be so insensitive? Was there no part of my life that was private anymore? Why should being the victim of an accident strip me of the right to dignity and compassion?* I couldn't wait to leave. Squirming in front of this medical lummox was unbearable.

Later I replayed that horrible conversation in my mind. I couldn't sleep that night. As I lay awake, staring at the ceiling, I took that doctor's grim prognosis as the last nail in the coffin of hope for my full recovery. *In hearing that the spinal surgery was a success and undertaking all the work of rehab with unbridled optimism, had I been kidding myself?* Until today, I had been convinced my accident was a temporary setback. *How could I have been so naive?*

Resignation and despair washed over me. It was ever more apparent that my once strong and capable body was likely gone forever. In its place was a weak and pathetic one, one whose prospect of living life fully as a woman was apparently gone, too. With hardly any feeling from the waist down, I could no longer leave home without catheters and medication. I had lost my bid as Australia's best hope for its women's Olympic ski team, and now my womanhood was being threatened as well. How much more could I bear losing?

I hated my body. I hated my life.

No longer able to hold back my emotions, I began to sob. There in the dark, encased in a plaster body cast, and barely able to move, I felt so alone, so helpless. *If I have to live the rest of my life like this, then maybe I don't want to live at all.* Over and over, I kept tormenting myself with the unanswerable question of why. When I had the choice back in the emergency room, why did I decide to return to this broken body?

I pulled myself to the edge of my bed and let myself fall to the floor. Lying there, I wiped the tears from my eyes and dragged myself to my knees. In desperation, I clasped my hands together in prayer and spoke aloud to the darkness:

"Please God," I begged, "show me a way through this, or show me a way out."

And then I let go.

PART TWO

REBUILDING A LIFE

If I can't walk, I'll fly.

› 14 ‹

Before my accident I had never thought of myself as an inventive person, but now I was about to embark on the most creative project any of us could ever undertake—rebuilding my life. Even though I had no idea what to do next, I was certain of one thing: I had hit rock bottom, and the pain of holding on to my former incarnation as a competitive athlete was too much to bear. Young and with my whole adult life ahead of me, I had to find something to replace what I had lost in my accident.

Ironically, uncertainty about my future brought a sense of freedom. No longer tied to a fixed path, I now had a clean slate with which to explore unlimited possibilities. That realization was about to change my life.

One afternoon while sitting outside and chatting with Mum, I heard the sound of a small plane and stopped mid-sentence to watch it pass overhead. As it disappeared into the distance, I was struck with the most unlikely idea.

"Hey, Mum. I think I'm going to learn to fly," I blurted.

"Oh that's nice, dear," she offered, unfazed. "But don't you think you should learn how to walk first?" Obviously, she'd taken my comment as an offhand remark, a joke, or a fanciful rambling.

"Mum, I'm not kidding. I really am going to learn to fly!"

This time, she paused, looking at me in disbelief. She recognized the determination in my eyes and knew I meant what I'd said.

"I can't walk properly, so why not fly? Besides, what else have I got to do at the moment? I can't sit around here forever."

I grew more taken with this far-fetched idea by the minute. With no prior interest or experience with small airplanes, I hadn't the faintest idea what I might be getting myself into, but the vision of flying suddenly intrigued me. Piloting an airplane, as unlikely as it seemed on the face of it, took hold as the thing I needed to get me back on my feet, so to speak.

"Mum, could you bring me the phone book?"

Still caught off-balance by this quirky twist in our conversation, she reluctantly obliged.

I flipped through the pages until I came to the heading, "Flying Schools." There were many, I was surprised to find, so I decided to try them alphabetically. I dialed the number of the first one, which started with "A." As the connection went through, I thought of what to say when someone answered, knowing that sooner or later, my disabilities would have to be revealed.

"Um, hello. I'm inquiring about flying lessons," I began.

"Of course," the voice responded. "You might be interested in our trial instructional flight, or TIF. We find an introductory lesson to be helpful. It lets people see if they really enjoy flying before they commit themselves."

"What does that involve?"

"After you register with us, we give you a briefing on what to expect for your first flight as a student pilot, and that lasts about half an hour. The instructor will let you take over and fly for a while, so you can see what it's all about."

"That sounds perfect," I said, my enthusiasm growing by the minute.

"I can book you in now if you like. We're at Bankstown Airport. When would you like to come out?"

I hesitated, and swallowed hard. I realized I hadn't thought things out quite this far.

"Um, well, that's a bit of a problem. I'm not sure yet. You see, I can't drive, and I sort of can't walk either . . ." I started to explain, but then deferred. "That's not a problem, is it?"

There was silence on the other end of the line. I held my breath and then continued. "I have a friend who'll drive me out. Can he come on the flight, too?" *What in the world must this person be thinking by now?*

"Well, sure, the plane is a four-seater, so there'll be plenty of room." With that assurance, the flight-school agent walked me through the details of booking a reservation.

As I hung up the phone, my mind was already racing. Chris, the long-time friend I was riding with on the day of my accident, was coming for a visit, and I was sure he'd be game for a flight.

In the short span since I'd had this idea, I'd grown nearly giddy with excitement at the prospect of flying. Though seemingly inconceivable for someone in my situation, the idea of piloting an airplane had consumed me. That the very thought of it was, after all, a little bit crazy just served to fuel my determination to at least give it a go. I needed to do something that was as far removed as possible from both my former and present lives—being a pilot certainly fit that bill. I had always risen to a challenge, and what better way to get fully engaged in living again than learning to fly?

Looking back, I realize that there was another key aspect to this seemingly random desire to become a pilot. Up to and including the day of my accident, I had built my entire world—and importantly, my circle of friends—around sports, defining myself through my excellence as a competitive athlete. Once I surrendered to accepting the extent of my injuries, there could be no return to the athletic world—and the thought of being relegated to the fringes of sports was too much to bear. While I didn't know if aviation would provide the foundation for beginning my life anew, one thing was certain: for someone with my physical limitations, training as a pilot certainly would be far removed from my present state.

Not surprisingly, Mum wasn't nearly as keen on the idea as I—not that I could blame her for having some apprehension, after what we had all just been through. But while she was concerned for my welfare, she also knew better than to say anything that might dampen my excitement. I imagine that when she heard the immediate lift in my spirits after my initial inquiry, Mum weighed this significant benefit against the small likelihood of possible risks.

When Chris arrived, and I told him what I had arranged, he shrugged and smiled, as if nothing I did ever surprised him. He proved to be as keen about the outing as I was. It turned out he'd always wanted to learn to fly, too.

On the day of our appointment, Chris drove me to Bankstown Airport, the region's designated general aviation facility. Struck with the realization of what I was about to do, I felt a twinge of nerves as we parked outside the school. I wondered what my doctors would say if they got wind of what I was up to so soon after being discharged.

Chris helped me out of his car, and with his arms firmly around me, he more or less carried me into the office of the flight school.

I was dressed in the same baggy jumpsuit Mum had bought me when I came home from the hospital. Even with its generous, flowing cut, my outfit failed to hide the body cast. As I waddled toward the building, holding onto Chris, I must have appeared a rather bulging, shapeless figure, most certainly not a former national ski champion or a future dashing pilot.

Chris held onto my arm as I shuffled to the counter. The two young men in pilot uniforms behind the desk eyed me warily, perhaps thinking I'd wandered in by mistake.

"Hi," I said with forced confidence. "My name is Janine Shepherd. I rang last week and booked a trial instructional flight."

There was a distinct hesitation before they excused themselves to check the schedule in a backroom. I imagined them drawing straws to see who would have to take me up.

One of them reappeared and extended his hand. "Hi, my name is Andrew, and I'll be taking you on your flight today," he said. He was smartly dressed in dark blue pants and a neat white pilot's shirt. He escorted Chris and me to the briefing room and explained in detail what we would be doing on the flight and a bit about the training course for a prospective pilot. He appeared young, but he behaved and spoke authoritatively. It seemed he knew what he was doing and could be trusted.

With the briefing and safety discussion accomplished, Andrew led us out to the tarmac. Although the instructional plane was parked only a little ways from the building, it was nonetheless farther than I could comfortably walk. Chris drove me as close as was practical in his car and then put his arms around me to help me manage the last few yards to the aircraft.

Our plane was much bigger than I had anticipated. It was a low-wing model of French manufacture called a Tobago. With a snazzy red-white-and-blue paint scheme, Andrew referred to it by the registration call sign emblazoned on its fuselage: JTO, or Juliet Tango Oscar in aviation's phonetic alphabet. My pulse raced as I eyed the fetching airplane I'd soon be flying.

There remained one imposing issue before we got to that though: how to get me in the cockpit. Entering the Tobago required stepping onto the wing and then down into the cabin. Both maneuvers were well beyond the limitations of my cast. It was decided that Chris and Andrew would lift me into the aircraft—though that, too, wasn't going to be made any easier by my cast. Chris positioned himself above me, and Andrew was at my feet. I can't imagine how the scene appeared to an observer, but somehow they managed to maneuver me onto the wing and into the plane.

Andrew settled into the other front seat and fastened the seatbelt for me since I couldn't reach the straps. I shot a glance at Chris in the back. I could sense that he was as excited as I was. Then I turned my gaze to the instrument panel, dazzled by what I saw. There were so many dials and switches. How could anyone ever keep track of them?

Andrew handed us each a pair of headsets, and with the flip of a switch, his voice came crackling through the earphones. I watched in fascination as he ticked off a series of checks and with a bit of flourish cleared the area for the engine start. Watching the propeller spin and hearing the engine rumble to life, I could hardly contain my anticipation. It was all so exciting!

"Okay, I'll explain how this all works," I heard Andrew say through the headphones. "This is the control column. Have a go at moving it for yourself."

I moved the control toward me and away, then left and right, as he directed. He took me through some of the other aircraft functions, one at a time, describing the purpose of each and how everything worked. When he came to the throttle, Andrew advanced it so that the engine revved up and the plane inched forward. As we taxied toward the runway, Andrew continued briefing us on the other controls.

"While on the ground, we steer the aircraft with our feet. Look at the floor and you'll see two pedals. By pushing with either my left or right foot, I can control direction and keep the aircraft following the painted line on the taxiway. Would you like to have a go?"

I didn't yet have the strength or control needed in my feet or legs—or any feeling in them. My heart sank. In my present condition, there was no way I could push the pedals with any hope of getting it right.

"That's a bit hard to reach with my plaster cast on, Andrew, so for the time being, let's give that a miss," I casually offered, neatly deflecting his request.

"Sure, that's fine," he reassured me.

We taxied along to what he called the run-up bay, where we stopped while Andrew went through numerous checks and procedures before takeoff. I glanced back and caught a reassuring smile on Chris's face.

For a moment, I closed my eyes and took stock of my life. Six months ago, I had a near-death experience from which I nearly didn't return, followed by more than five months spent in a spinal ward. It wasn't clear whether I'd ever walk again, yet I was moments from takeoff in an airplane *where I would be at the controls*. It was both a daunting and magical thought.

All checks completed to our instructor's satisfaction, we taxied to the runway hold line and awaited instructions from the control tower for further clearance. It wasn't long before the controller's voice came through the radio, "Juliet Tango Oscar, cleared for takeoff."

Andrew replied to acknowledge the clearance and smoothly advanced the throttle. As the engine revved to full power, we accelerated. I watched spellbound as the pavement flashed beneath us and everything beyond the plane blurred with increasing speed. We lifted off into a clear blue sky. As we climbed, I felt a fluttering in my stomach, but as I looked down at the world below with awe, I realized it was just butterflies. Indeed, I was smitten. It was the most incredible experience, no longer feeling confined by the limitations of my injuries. I was flying!

We reached 3,000 feet as we arrived over an area designated for student training. The sky was dazzlingly clear, and I could see all the way to the distant horizon. Everything seemed so tiny from our lofty perch far above the Sydney skyline. The iconic Opera House and Harbour Bridge were visible in the distance. Andrew's voice interrupted my reverie and brought me back to the cockpit.

"Okay, Janine. Now it's your turn," Andrew said. "Remember to try to hold a straight heading." He gave me the agreed-upon cue for transfer of control—"handing over"—and I cautiously gripped the wheel.

"See that mountain?" he asked, pointing at the horizon. "I'd like you to steer the aircraft toward that."

As I focused on keeping the plane "straight and level," I was struck by the plane's sensitivity to any movement in response to my control input. More than that, though, I was absolutely giddy about piloting an airplane for the first time. What a thrill!

I continued to fly toward the mountain, as instructed. I was so intent that it took me a bit before I recognized the irony of my aim point. I'd been directed to steer the aircraft toward the Blue Mountain Range, the very place where I'd had my accident! It dawned on me how incredible this moment was and the special significance of what was intended to be a simple introductory flight lesson. I was elated, nearly to the point of tears, and for the time being, any concerns for my recovery seemed as far away as that mountain.

After months of hearing so many medical experts, well-meaning friends, and counselors tell me what I could and couldn't do, I had discovered the one thing that I wanted to do. I recognized that familiar feeling of competence and confidence I'd felt in my days as an athlete. In a moment of clear synchronicity, I knew one thing with complete certainty: I was going to learn to fly!

All too soon we turned back to the airport. Andrew landed the plane and taxied back to the ramp. In the debriefing room, I thanked him for the flight and asked what I needed to do to get a license. One of the first things, he offered gingerly, would be to pass a pilot's medical exam. Gauging from his hesitation, it was apparent this exam would present a problem, but I dismissed it. I had overcome tougher challenges. He further explained that I would have to pass a few written and oral exams as my lessons progressed toward the final "check ride," the practical test. All of the required ground study for licensing was covered in instructional manuals. The practical preparation we'd tackle one flight at a time.

With that, we shook hands and bid each other goodbye. I suspected that Andrew thought he would never see me again. But that TIF proved to me I was ready to start my aviation studies. As we drove away, I asked Chris to stop at the airport pilot shop, where I bought the entire set of course manuals for the private pilot's license on the spot.

Books in hand, I was determined not to waste any time. Though I knew nothing about flying—the study of which included the subjects of physics, weather, aircraft systems, and regulations—I vowed to start with the same commitment I'd given to athletic training before my accident. Rehab, too, would see redoubled effort, to accelerate my progress so that I'd be fit enough to make my best showing for the medical exam.

› 15 ‹

The day finally arrived to have my body cast replaced with a custom-designed brace. Besides being lighter and less rigid, the new brace was intended to perform more like an open supporting frame. At last, my skin could breathe! Best of all, my range of motion would be much less limited than it had been in the cumbersome cast.

The attending physicians and I were relieved to find the brace, built from our measurements, fit perfectly. Freed from my plaster encasement, I couldn't wait to take a shower—my first in seven months. I was allowed to remove the brace for the shower, as long as I kept my back straight and took great care not to fall. Mum prepared things accordingly, placing a chair in the shower, both for stability and as a resting spot should my legs tire.

I undressed and removed my brace. Naked and nervous, I took firm hold of the chair and glanced down at the rest of my body for the first time since my accident. My heart sank. Once I'd possessed the chiseled physique of an athlete, but now hip bones protruded and ribs poked out like the bars of a cage. I reached down and ran my hand along the scar that wrapped around my torso, an indelible reminder of how much my world had changed.

Assessing the emaciated state of my body, I felt shaky and vulnerable. It was the first time I had stood without back support since the accident, and it was unnerving. A fall now could undo all I'd gained through weeks of rehab—even worse, it could confine me to a wheelchair. The very thought caused my grip to tighten on the arms of the chair. I could imagine the stress on the still weak bones in my back. I hoped they wouldn't give way under the strain of supporting my weight as I stood without the brace. Though I trusted Dr. Stephen's protocol in allowing me the luxury of a shower, discretion was in order for the first one. So instead of standing, I sat on the chair as I opened the taps.

As the soothing water streamed down my body, I closed my eyes and lifted my head, letting the water stream onto my face and savoring its warmth. I was so transfixed by sensations that I stayed in the shower for over half an hour, delighting in the sheer pleasure of something so simple and yet so luxurious.

That night I was treated to another joyful "first"—going to bed without my brace. The shower was an indulgence, but it paled in comparison to the freedom of sleeping unencumbered by a cast or a metal frame. Even the simplest moves, like being able to roll over, were sheer bliss.

Now that I was gaining physical independence, I resolved to undertake my rehabilitation on my own. I'd reached the limits of what the hospital could offer. Besides, I was experienced and knowledgeable enough in physical fitness training to be confident designing and executing my own regimen. My medical team agreed and wished me the best, offering me the option to return as needed. I had a plan, though, and I wasn't about to look back.

I began my daily routine with a lap swim. Like so many other activities I'd readily participated in before my accident, even a swim now required careful thought to logistics and my still-mending bones. I chose an indoor pool for the first outing because it was less crowded and that reduced the chance of my being bumped by a careless swimmer—a prospect that terrified me.

As to the detailed requirements of my swim training, they were myriad. First, I would change into my swimsuit at home and then put my brace and tracksuit over it. When we arrived at the pool, Mum had to help me undress and remove the brace. Relying on her tight grip around my waist, I'd waddle to the edge of the pool, choosing each foot plant carefully to guard against a slip. Mum stayed on high alert too, with a firm hold on me until I grasped the railing along the steps at the pool's edge. Measured step by measured step, in slow motion, I lowered myself into the water.

The first time I went swimming, I was overwhelmed by the delightful sensation of being immersed in water. Weightless and free-floating, I stretched out my arms, closed my eyes, and basked in the moment. Oh God, how I had missed this!

All right. Enough of this luxury. I let my feet drift down to the bottom and tried to stand on my toes, counting on the buoyancy of the water to help me lift myself. Still, no luck. The nerves in my calves and feet refused to respond to the command.

I shifted my attention to the lane ahead of me. "I think I'll try a few laps," I called to Mum, who watched me like a hawk.

"Don't you think you should do some basic warm-up exercises before you try something so strenuous?"

"Oh, I'll be all right. I'll go slowly."

With that, I pushed off from the side of the pool. Starting with a freestyle stroke to keep my back straight, I moved my arm up and over my head to discover . . . *I can still swim!* My arms were stronger than I'd thought, and though my legs floundered ineffectively, it didn't matter because I compensated with the powerful pull from my upper body.

Then a new challenge arose. After a few strokes, I remembered that I would have to take a breath soon, the prospect of which gave me pause. I'd been told that my broken neck had fully healed, but turning it nearly ninety degrees would be the first test of that much range of motion. Would my fragile, once-broken neck be okay? The reflex need for oxygen forced the decision. I lifted my head to the side and gulped the fresh air, turned my head back to alignment, and continued swimming. Another test passed! I smiled underwater.

When I reached the opposite end of the pool, I turned around for the return. Surprisingly, thus far, swimming was almost effortless. Breathing came easily, and my arm muscles could handle the load. Perhaps I hadn't lost as much fitness as I'd feared. So what about another, just to see if I could do it? To my delight, I did it again with not all that much effort. Encouraged, I kept going, wanting to see how long I'd last. I continued to swim, lap after lap. Before long, I'd logged twenty return trips, and then I thought it best to rest.

When I reached her end of the pool at the last round, Mum's stern gaze told me that by her measure I was pushing too hard for my first swim.

I glanced at my watch and stopped the timer. Gauging by the elapsed time, my laps had been slow, but I had established a starting point from which to measure progress.

"And what do you think you're doing now?" Mum demanded, unable any longer to contain her concern.

"Oh, I wanted to know my pace at the start of my training, so I can set some targets for improving."

"I think you might be overdoing it, don't you?" she said, her tone growing stern.

"No, I'm fine. How did I look?"

"Great! But let's do call it a day. You can do more tomorrow. Come on, I'll help you out."

Twenty laps—not a bad start. But the next time I resolved to try for more and to decrease my interval times.

At home, I showered, changed, and then sat down to begin a new page in my training log. During ski training I always kept a record of my workouts and results. I decided that setting targets for rehab and recovery should be no different. Having good data on my progress would also help me spot any areas of potential weakness, so I could fine-tune my rehab program. More importantly, though, I depended on *seeing* each incremental gain in physical strength and endurance to feed my motivation and help me dig deeper with each session.

Before making that first entry, I flipped back to previous ones in the log, curious about sessions recorded the week before my accident. My record-keeping had been meticulous: notes of hours slept each night, my resting heart rate, and other indicators of how my body was handling the intensive training regimen. Day after day, I'd filled the columns with precise notes on all of my activities. The pages starting with May 31st were blank. I paused for a moment as I considered the months of missing entries and then wrote in the blank spot by that day: "ACCIDENT!"

I turned to a new page and began afresh: "Day one with my plaster off. Shower and swim. 500 meters. Pool crowded. Felt fantastic." Then I added, "YIPPEE!"

When I woke the following morning, I immediately checked my heart rate: 58. In my career as a competitive athlete, a resting pulse this high would have indicated overtraining or impending illness—my usual at the time would have been around 38. Considering what I had been through, 58 wasn't bad, although I resolved to lower it. At the pool that morning, I managed to double the previous day's swim and log one kilometer. It felt so natural to be in the water, and the fact that I could now exercise free of the constricting brace was a tremendous boost to my spirits.

By the end of the second week of my program, I'd reached two significant milestones: my resting pulse had lowered to 48, and I was sleeping longer and with less interruption. In this short time, I grew strong enough in the pool to introduce intervals into my sessions—short bursts of all-out effort. My legs were still weak. I vowed to concentrate on my kicking technique and spend more time stretching to stimulate lower body recovery.

Mum and I settled into my new training routine. She would drop me off at the pool, and I'd tick off my planned regimen for that day. After a warm-up of twenty laps, I would do "bunny hops" at the shallow end of the pool, followed by some striding and running, exercises aimed at strengthening my legs. That was the magic of the pool: I couldn't run on dry land, but supported by the water's buoyancy, I could do most anything. Next, I'd log at least twenty laps by kicking only, hoping to gain mobility in my feet and ankles. Finally, I'd use hand paddles as added resistance for the remaining laps so that I didn't neglect my upper body.

Back at home I would spend time after lunch on an exercise bike. It had been loaned to me by a thoughtful college lecturer, Peter, who with my other classmates and teachers continued to support my recovery efforts. I would dress in proper riding gear to look the part of a cyclist, which started me in the right frame of mind for the session. The bike was set up in front of the mirror so I could watch myself and improve my technique—a rehab protocol I'd learned from the hospital. I wore the same heart-rate monitor I had used for ski training and modulated the intensity of my workout according to the readings. Taking my training program seriously gave me a sense of purpose. Setting, reaching, and re-setting goals continued to be a key metric in my desire to regain normalcy.

As I gained strength and confidence, I decided that at least twice a day I would add in some aerobics and weight exercises. I collected the tapes from the aerobics classes I'd taught previously, only now I'd sit on the floor to perform whatever parts of the routine I could manage with my injuries. Day after day, with sweat dripping from my brow, I struggled to perform what before my accident had been the simplest of motions, but the challenges only strengthened my resolve.

I kept at it and made modest gains, but my training wasn't without struggle. At times I'd get discouraged and miss the feeling of my body moving effortlessly and powerfully. I'd wonder how I would ever regain my strength. When I had a down day, I would look back over my notes to remind myself of the progress I'd already made. That always helped me to find the motivation to get back on track and redouble my effort.

Days became weeks, then months, and I began to see measurable, albeit still limited progress in my overall mobility. To me, the improvement was so minute as to be hardly noticeable; to Mum it was clear how much more easily I was getting around the house, and how much less halting were my movements. Her acknowledgment of my recovery and unflagging encouragement were great boosts to my morale.

There was one area where even I agreed there had been significant improvement, and that was walking. I had progressed from being supported by someone else, to using the furniture as a brace, to using the walls to supplement balance. Mum joked that when I used that latest tactic, she had to follow me around, wiping the trail of dirty fingerprints I left behind, but at least she always knew where she could find me!

Once I'd progressed to a point of relying on only minimal aid, I decided it was time I learned to walk without any support whatsoever. This would be no small task for a partial paraplegic with impaired lower-leg and foot function. My progression began with a few steps on my own, as I negotiated my way between opportunities for support. To do this, I first sized up the gap between two pieces of furniture and estimated the number of steps required to cross without assistance. Readying myself, I'd launch from my starting place and hurtle across from, say, chair to table and back to the wall again. On occasion, I would misjudge things and teeter, but I made sure there was always another piece of furniture nearby for safety. Learning to walk this way wasn't the most coordinated or graceful process to observe, but it proved effective in incrementally reducing my reliance on support.

When I wasn't swimming, lifting weights, cycling, or practicing walking, I had my head buried in the training manuals for my pilot's license. Never before had I shown the least bit of interest in things like aerodynamics or the intricacies of how an engine and propeller create thrust. But now, these and other applied aviation studies became the very subjects I had to get on top of to qualify as a pilot.

Most applicants for a pilot's license attend a course at a technical college or flight school to accomplish the ground portion of their required training. I still couldn't drive or sit for an extended time in a classroom, so it fell to me to undertake my ground school studies independently. Although at times I struggled to understand certain technical aspects of the courses, my immersion in this self-directed coursework was a welcome respite from the physical and emotional challenges of recovery.

Even without going to a classroom, all the time I spent poring over the books led to another challenge stemming from my injuries: I found it distressing to sit in one place for long. My back and neck would ache, and the body brace was uncomfortable and constricting. Add to that my tendency to tire and the limited attention span from head trauma, and the attempt to navigate complicated and technical new subject matter proved to be a mental struggle. Still, I had a goal. As with my physical training, the prospect of successfully achieving something worthwhile was motivation enough to help me push beyond the physical discomfort.

With practice, my unaided walking improved, and I could manage a few steps on my own, albeit with a distinctive waddle. I had yet to regain nerve function or sensation in my legs and buttocks, so I still needed to hold on to someone for support for longer distances. Casting aside the concerns that came with these limitations, I decided it was as good a time as any to apply for my flight physical, since the practical training for my pilot's license depended on the outcome of that exam.

The flight school had given me the phone number of a doctor authorized by the Civil Aviation Authority (CAA) to examine pilot applicants. Dr. Henderson's office wasn't far from home, so Mum drove me there for my appointment. Sporting baggy overalls to camouflage my brace, I hobbled into his waiting room, leaning on Mum's arm for support. I smiled to myself, wondering what the doctor's first impressions might be. I was hardly the usual future pilot applicant, and with my mother in tow at that.

We waited for what seemed an eternity until at last the examining room door opened. An elderly man emerged, wearing a lab coat, a stethoscope, and a clichéd pair of spectacles perched on the end of his nose. "Hello. You must be Janine," he said pleasantly. "Please come inside."

Mum gave me a boost to stand and then helped me waddle into his examining room. Out of the corner of my eye, I saw Dr. Henderson take notice of the odd way I walked. *Here we go. This ought to be good.*

The walls of the examining room were decorated with photographs of airplanes. I wondered if he was a pilot.

"Now," he began, and then hesitated, "you said you were here for a *flight* physical?"

"Yes, that's right," I replied, feigning confidence.

He looked up at me, peering over his glasses at the metal frame poking out from under my clothes.

"Are you wearing a brace?" he asked, sounding ever more incredulous.

"Um . . . yes . . . I am."

"Well, then," he began, removing his glasses to underscore the effect of his stern look, "perhaps you had better tell me what this is all about."

"Well, I was in an accident, hit by a truck while I was riding my bike."

"Goodness me," he replied sympathetically. "Well, now, that's not very nice, is it? What injuries did you sustain?" He began to make notes on the form that was to become my medical exam record.

"Um, there were quite a few. Let's see, I broke my neck and back, I broke my arm, five ribs . . ." I continued through the all-too-familiar inventory of injuries. By the time I finished, he had already put down his pen and was peering at me with a look of amazement.

"That's quite a lot." He sighed. "Maybe we should start at the beginning. Tell me about the accident."

Dr. Henderson listened intently as I recounted the last six months. It was evident he hadn't seen anyone with my medical history on her way to becoming a pilot, but it soon became equally clear he was keen to help me as best he could.

When at last I finished, he looked at me as if pondering what next to say or do.

"Have you been up in an airplane before?" he asked at last.

"Oh, yes!" I answered, with a fresh flush of optimism. "I went for a trial instructional flight a few months ago, and I loved it. I've been spending all my time since then doing rehabilitation so that I'd be strong enough to pass a medical. And I've been studying the pilot manuals as well. I want to fly, and I'm confident I'll make a good pilot." My response ended with a hint of a plea.

Hearing my enthusiasm, kind Dr. Henderson began to tell me of his experiences and how flying was one of his great passions. He went on to offer how he could no longer fly because of health issues and how much he missed it. Aviation, he stressed, was a wonderful pastime, and he believed that everyone interested should try it, even someone with my injuries.

I breathed a sigh of relief. Thank goodness my medical examiner was proving to be an ally.

"Well, I guess if we are going to examine you, we'd better begin," he said with a chuckle. "Let's start with the paperwork." He handed me a form to fill in from the CAA:

> Have you ever had an operation?
> Was the operation recent? If yes, how long ago?
> Have you ever had a head injury?
> Have you ever broken any bones?

The list went on to relentlessly flush out all the physical issues stemming from my accident. By the time I'd worked my way through the form, I had checked "yes" to nearly every affliction. Looking over the marked-up form made me feel like a medical freak. *How could any physical exam ever pronounce me fit enough to pilot a plane?*

With a lump in my throat, I handed the checklist to Dr. Henderson, who dutifully studied my replies, emitting a soft "Hmm" when he came across something especially deserving of remark. Finally, he put the form down, took off his glasses, and let out a hearty laugh. "Well, our medical associates at Civil Aviation Authority in Canberra are going to have fun reading this! Let's get on with the rest of the examination, shall we?"

With that he started the practical part of the flight physical, which I feared would prove more challenging than the application form. For a start, he asked me to perform what for any other applicant would be a simple warm-up exercise: stand in one spot and march as a test of balance. Because I could barely walk, let alone do what he was asking, I did some quick thinking and came up with a resourceful option. I shuffled over to the bed and leaned against it until I could feel the frame behind me, then I braced against it. My sleight of hand was too subtle for Dr. Henderson to catch, though to ensure success, I continued to chat him up, hoping he wouldn't notice my makeshift crutch. My subterfuge did the trick. He ticked that box and moved on to the next test.

He produced a rubber-tipped instrument, a reflex hammer, and began to tap my knee. This is a common test of nerve response to stimulation, so I wasn't surprised when my leg didn't get the message. Seeing no reason why a lack of a knee jerk from a hammer should stop me from flying an aircraft, I faked it. I moved my lower leg ever so slightly to mimic the response he was looking for. Another box ticked.

On we went. Many of the subsequent tests required similar creativity on my part. After an hour, we finished, though he added the stipulation of a letter of blessing from Dr. Stephen, my primary surgeon. Even with that, Dr. Henderson warned, a question mark might well remain over my being allowed to undertake the pilot training course.

The exam over, Dr. Henderson wished me luck, saying he would endorse the medical I needed to pursue my license. Another doctor might well have rejected me outright, but Dr. Henderson, a pilot and an aviation enthusiast, was willing to give me the chance to prove myself. To this day, I remain grateful to him for that, although

I also know he wouldn't have done so without faith in my abilities and determination.

I went straightaway to see Dr. Stephen. "Well, Janine, what have you been up to of late?" he said as we sat down in his office. "You look to be walking well."

"Thanks. I've been working out every day, swimming and doing weights and practicing my balance. I'm much stronger."

He nodded his approval.

"Oh, and my brace is an improvement, too. The plaster cast was driving me mad." I laughed, underscoring my progress while I used small talk to appear nonchalant.

"Well, we'd better have a look at you then." He helped me over to a bed where he inspected the brace and my back.

"Okay," he said. "Let's see you walk a bit. Just go over to the door."

I took a few tentative steps, then turned around and came back.

"That's amazing," he said with conviction. "I'm impressed with the way you've compensated for the muscles you've lost in your legs. If you don't mind, I'd like a colleague to have a look."

Dr. Stephen summoned his associate from the room next door, and together they observed me waddle up and down the hallway. I didn't let on at the tremendous concentration it took to stay upright. I moved slowly, and my feet flopped all over the place—but I did my utmost to make it look effortless.

Back in Dr. Stephen's room, with his pleasure at my progress evident, I decided to be direct. "Dr. Stephen, there's something else I wanted to talk about with you today."

"Yes, Janine, what is it now?" he asked, wryly.

"Well, I have decided to learn to fly. I went for my medical, and the doctor said that he would pass me. But the aviation authorities will require a letter from you giving me the okay."

He looked at me quizzically at first and then smiled. "Well, nothing you do would shock me, Janine. What on earth put that idea into your head?"

"Well, I needed to find some new challenge, and I think aviation might be the answer. Since I took my trial instructional flight, I've been digging into the training manuals. I love it."

As it turned out, Dr. Stephen had done some flying, too, which gave us the opportunity to chat more personally about aviation and my interest. So far, everything was working in my favor.

"The thing that worries me is your legs," he said with sincere concern. "How will you operate the rudder pedals?"

"Oh, I have that covered. I'm doing exercises all the time to strengthen my legs, and my instructor will help with the pedals until I'm strong enough on my own. They'll be fine. Believe me, Dr. Stephen." Then I added with sincere emotion, "*Please* say it's okay."

He paused, appearing to give the request due consideration, then took a piece of paper from his desk and began writing: *To whom it may concern* . . . . His letter described my medical history and the operation he had performed on my back and spine. It went on to say that he saw no reason why I shouldn't hold a pilot's license.

I exhaled as he handed me the key to my pilot medical and wished me the best of luck. I thanked him and assured him I'd keep him apprised of my progress. With a flourish of heartfelt confidence, I promised that one day I'd be able to take him up for a ride. He smiled. With his letter in hand, there was just one more hurdle: approval from the Civil Aviation Authority.

Once my medical application and supporting letters had been submitted to Canberra, I contacted Andrew, the flight instructor, with the news that I had passed my medical. I was delighted when he pointed out that I was allowed to clock up a few hours of flight time even before being issued the student's license that came with official CAA medical approval. The prospect of putting my studies into practice sounded fantastic, so I booked my first lesson.

When I arrived at the flying school on my first day, I felt decidedly out of place. I couldn't tell the flight instructors from the students, but to a person they all seemed to be staring at me. Not that staring was unexpected. I was gaunt, wearing brightly colored overalls, and the corners of my brace protruded from my unorthodox clothing. Everyone else was dressed in what seemed to be the mandatory airport garb of blue pants and a white shirt.

Appearance aside, it took my utmost concentration to balance on my unsteady legs. When I walked, my feet dragged underneath me, while my upper body remained stiff, which made it look as though I might tumble at any moment. I periodically had to grab onto anything—or anyone—nearby to rest or to regain my balance.

At first my clothing and unsteadiness made me self-conscious. Even though I felt somewhat embarrassed by the way people stared, I shrugged it off, focusing only on getting through each flight. I reckoned that once I was at the controls of the aircraft, I would be on equal footing, as it were, with any other student in the school—though I resolved to achieve a level of excellence in both preparation and performance that would place me at the top of the class.

Andrew greeted me, "Would you like a cup of tea or coffee before we start?"

"That would be nice. Thanks."

"I'll show you where it is. Feel free to make yourself a cup whenever you want."

The kitchen was in the corner of a large room that held a couple of tables with a dozen or so chairs around them. "This is the crew room, for the pilots' use, and over there are the briefing rooms," Andrew explained, pointing to a row of doors.

After making a cup of tea for me and coffee for himself, Andrew led me into one of the briefing rooms for a preview of the day's lesson. The blackboard on the wall was covered with diagrams from a previous instructor, and posters of planes were pinned up on every available section of the walls. Andrew took out his notes and got down to business.

"Right. Today's lesson is 'Effects of Controls,'" he said, writing the words on the chalkboard for emphasis. I dutifully took a pen and paper out of my handbag and began taking notes.

Using a model plane, Andrew explained each of the control surfaces of an aircraft. I followed intently and with complete understanding, pleased with my level of recall on this subject from my studies of the training manuals. We covered both the primary and secondary effects of these controls, how they were operated from the cockpit, and where they were located on the airframe. He then explained the effects of airspeed, some aspects of the ancillary controls, and closed his presentation with basic points of elementary airmanship.

Next he briefed me on some safety aspects of our flight lesson. If he used the expression "handing over" once airborne, it was my turn to fly. Similarly, any time he said "taking over," I was to relinquish the controls to him immediately and without question. Thus there would be no misunderstanding about who was piloting the plane at any time—a critical point for both instructor and student to agree upon.

Andrew cautioned me that the Bankstown flight training area stayed busy, so it was important to keep a good lookout for other aircraft while we were engaged in our maneuvers. Finally, he gave me some introductory notes on the plane we would be flying, a model called Tampico.

The briefing took about forty-five minutes, by which time I had absorbed quite a lot of information. I was also reaching my limit of sitting in one place, so I was relieved when he said it was time to go fly. The tarmac where the aircraft was parked was a long way for me to walk, but I was careful to conceal this challenge from Andrew.

Sporting the registration JTL (Juliet Tango Lima), the aircraft we'd use for this first instructional flight was a brown and white machine that looked a bit shopworn even from a distance. Once we had inspected the plane, the "walk around" as it was called, I realized it was going to be tricky getting into the pilot's seat with the limitations posed by my brace. It was a real knock to my pride to admit that I couldn't manage something on my own, but here I had no choice. If I wanted to fly, I had to have some help getting in, and I was grateful to Andrew when he offered it.

After giving me a hand with securing my safety belt, Andrew began reciting his checklist of the things to be inspected or confirmed before starting the engine. To teach me the process, he'd point to a particular switch or lever and direct me to carry out the appropriate procedure with each. There was so much to do. I wondered how anyone could ever remember it all, and I quickly learned to appreciate the value of the printed checklist.

Pre-start inspection completed, Andrew yelled the warning "Clear prop" to any passersby and turned the ignition key. With a cough and a sputter, the engine turned the propeller until it spun at a steady idle speed. We put our headsets on and carried out pre-taxi checks. Andrew and I listened to the radio frequency that broadcast a recorded briefing on wind direction, preferred runway, and other important departure information. He then tuned the radio to air traffic control and told them we were prepared to taxi for a flight to the training area.

Advancing the throttle, Andrew pressed the floor pedals to swing the plane around and to set us off down the taxiway. When he suggested I have a try, I demurred, explaining I needed to strengthen my feet and legs a bit more before I could actuate the rudder pedals with the force needed to safely taxi the plane.

We arrived at a wide spot in the taxiway, just shy of the runway threshold, called the run-up bay. This was the designated holding area where we'd do our pre-takeoff checks. Andrew confirmed that the engine was operating to standards and that the instruments and controls were configured for departure. Satisfied that all was okay, we made our way to the runway.

With another call to the control tower, we received permission to line up and await takeoff clearance. My excitement and anticipation growing by the second, it seemed like an eternity before that magical moment would come. Finally, I heard a voice through the headsets: "Juliet Tango Lima cleared for takeoff."

Andrew acknowledged our clearance and directed me to put one hand on the control column, with my other on the throttle. As I advanced the throttle, JTL accelerated until we roared along the runway. I had my eyes fixed on the centerline, not daring to look to the side. Everything seemed to be happening so quickly.

"Okay. Start adding back pressure by pulling gently on the control column," Andrew said, and with that, the airplane lifted off the ground. We had taken off. No, *I* had taken off! The pavement disappeared beneath us, and the windscreen was filled with blue sky and puffy white clouds. As we climbed, I focused my gaze ahead, remembering Andrew's admonishment to always be on lookout for other small aircraft.

Soon we arrived at the designated training area. "Now, let's manipulate each of the primary controls we talked about," Andrew said, adding the required "Taking over" as he assumed command. He went on to demonstrate the various points we had discussed in the classroom, first under his control, then commanding "Handing over" for me to have a go at each. It all flowed logically, and the lesson connected many of the points about aerodynamics that I had been studying.

I couldn't help but be exhilarated sitting in the pilot's seat, in my body brace, with legs that didn't even work properly, yet at the controls of an aircraft in flight! How I wished my doctors and friends from the acute spinal ward could see me now. Not even a broken body could stop me from appreciating the beauty and magic of flight.

Our first instructional session passed too quickly. Andrew had me "follow through" (touching but not moving the controls) as he deftly landed JTL. We taxied back to the flight school to debrief over another cup of tea.

By the time Mum arrived to pick me up, I had already booked my next instructional session. I was determined to get as many lessons under my belt as I could before CAA rendered its decision about my application—just in case my application was denied.

In the weeks before my next lesson, I would read as much as I could absorb, to be best prepared for each flight. And I resolved to step up my exercises and rehab training in hopes of regaining the strength I needed in my feet and legs to taxi the plane. With set goals to focus on, I had all the incentive I needed to push myself even harder.

> 16 <

My next lesson proceeded like the first—the cup of tea, a briefing, note taking, and the shuffling walk to the airplane. Accommodating my physical limitations, Andrew graciously excused me from the pre-flight inspections—that could come later once I regained more mobility.

When I got home that day, December 22, an official-looking envelope from Canberra bearing the CAA's insignia was waiting for me. I reckoned it was the decision on my medical. What if they had rejected me? I held my breath as I tore open the envelope with a mix of excitement and dread. I scanned it eagerly until I came to:

Student Pilot License . . . approved.

My heart leapt! Despite the odds stacked against me, I had received the medical permission required to become a pilot. Just this small milestone seemed as important as if I had won an Olympic Gold Medal. It wasn't that long ago when a doctor in the hospital had told me I would never be able to do the things I did before. Well, she was partly right. I wouldn't be going to the Olympics as a ski racer, but then again, she hadn't considered that I might choose instead to pilot an aircraft!

I telephoned the flight school to tell them the good news and to book a lesson two days hence. Most people would have been planning celebrations on Christmas Eve, but I wanted to squeeze in one more flight before the school closed for the holidays.

My first Christmas after the accident brought with it conflicting emotions. Although thrilled to be out of the spinal ward and to be home with my family, I was also deeply saddened by the thought of not being overseas skiing with the Australian National Team.

Two weeks after Christmas was my twenty-fifth birthday. Mum decided to throw a big party for me, thinking friends and family might help boost my spirits. I had an appointment with Dr. Stephen the week before that, and I pleaded with him to let me dispense with my brace in time for the celebration Mum was planning. I was relieved when he agreed.

As soon as I got home, I took the wretched thing off and tossed it out of sight. Free at last! I took a few halting steps around my room, savoring my newfound freedom but at the same time feeling vulnerable and unprotected. Now I could anticipate the last remaining steps in my return to normalcy: dressing in clothes that fit, diving full-on into training and recovery unhindered by that brace, and most exciting of all, advancing my flight training schedule. But the very first thing I longed to do was take a bath, a simple pleasure I'd been dreaming about since my accident.

Mum filled the tub for me, and in I stepped. Although the water was hot, the lack of sensation in my legs and buttocks meant I couldn't gauge the temperature until I sat down. Instinctively flinching as I first sensed the temperature reminded me how much of my body was still numb. I sat upright in the bath, hesitant to bend my back. But then what good was a bath if you couldn't lie down? I lowered my upper body into the tub, clutching the sides for security. The soothing warm water enveloped me. I closed my eyes and sank into bliss.

On the day of my birthday party, a crowd turned up, although most of my athlete friends were training and skiing overseas. Daven was traveling with his racing team, so his family came instead. As with all my visitors in the hospital, I was grateful for the outpouring of love and support. Mum had prepared a veritable feast, crowned by a huge birthday cake inscribed "Happy 25th Birthday, Janine" in bold letters. After everyone had gathered around the table and sung a hearty "Happy Birthday," Dad asked to say a few words.

Normally he was reserved, but his voice wavered with emotion as he expressed his gratitude for the generous support offered to our family since the accident. Finally overcome, he paused in mid-speech, fighting back tears in a futile attempt to maintain his composure. There wasn't a dry eye in the room, least of all mine. As I scanned the familiar, loving faces gathered to celebrate the day I was born, I was struck by how fortunate I was to be here at all. I had been given a second chance at life, albeit a different one, and that realization made this birthday celebration one of the most special.

Now that my brace was off, there were a million "normal" things I wanted to do. My top priority was to get behind the wheel of my car. As much as I appreciated the kindness of friends and family chauffeurs, I longed for the independence of being able to drive once again.

As with so many things about my post-accident condition, I faced a challenge as a driver. My car had a manual transmission, requiring me to engage the clutch pedal with one foot in order to change gears. But my legs remained weak, and I was still nagged by poor proprioception. I wasn't sure I'd be able to find the clutch without looking down to assure foot placement, which is never a good idea when driving.

I knew my desire to be back on the road so soon would alarm Mum, so I waited until she was at work before having a go at driving. The car was parked in our driveway. I swallowed hard, put the keys in the ignition, and started the engine. With great care, I set aside my concerns and placed my left foot on the clutch pedal. To my delight and relief, I found I could move it. First hurdle overcome. I put the car into gear, and it lurched forward. First I drove it up the driveway and then backed in again, daring to move a bit farther with each change of direction. All that remained before hitting the open road was for me to adjust my shifting to get the timing right. With my impaired reflexes, that required some practice.

Our home was on a quiet street with little traffic during the workday. At the end of the driveway, I confirmed the coast was clear and pulled into the street. Without sensation in my legs, I had to make my best guess in timing clutch and accelerator inputs. So, rather than shift just yet, I made my way up the street in fits and starts by staying in first gear. What a curious sight that must have been for the neighbors!

Emboldened by my success, I decided to continue my way around the block. As I turned the corner, I took the plunge into second gear. At first, I had to steal the occasional glance at the floorboard to confirm the placement of my feet, but soon I connected with my motor-memory skills and driving became more natural. I went around the block again, and then a third time, until I got the hang of smoothly changing the gears.

I managed to park the car back in the driveway before Mum came home. I wasn't sure how she'd accept the news that I'd been experimenting with driving so soon. But she agreed, albeit grudgingly, to let me take her for a few laps around the block until she was satisfied I wouldn't do any harm to the car, myself, or anyone else.

Getting my wheels back was a tremendous stepping-stone for my recovery, as well as serving to progress my flying skills. I no longer had to rely on others to shuttle me back and forth, and I could go to the airport more often. Fueled by both my ambition and newfound freedom, the pace of my flight lessons quickened—sometimes I logged two flights a day. Using my legs to drive yielded another benefit: I found I could transfer my driving skills to operating the rudder pedals on the floor of the cockpit. With a great deal of concentration and all of my strength, I was soon able to keep the plane tracking straight down the taxiway without Andrew's assistance.

Because the wheel brakes on most light airplanes are activated by depressing the top of the rudder pedals, I needed to work out not only how to control speed when taxiing but also how to stop. I still couldn't move the pedals the normal way; instead, I had to push with my heels, drawing on the strength of my less-impaired thighs. To gain additional leverage, I placed a pillow behind my back to slide my feet closer to the rudder controls.

Once I could manage the aircraft from engine start to shutdown unaided, my training advanced to the "circuits" level in my syllabus. Flying circuits meant executing takeoffs and landings in repeated succession while remaining in the airport's approach pattern. With circuits came a demanding workload in very little time: managing flight and engine controls, completing checks, calling air traffic control for instructions, and all while watching out for the numerous other aircraft in the area. With practice, I gained proficiency and confidence in this, too, and circuits soon became second nature.

On January 17, I turned up for a circuit session and learned I'd be flying with a different instructor that day, Bill. No matter. It was a perfect day to practice. The sun was shining, and there wasn't much traffic in the circuit area. I did my best to demonstrate my competency in takeoffs and landings to my new instructor. Everything seemed to be going well. So I was surprised when Bill asked me to taxi clear of the runway after a couple of circuits.

With a sidelong glance at me, he picked up the microphone to call the controller. "Bankstown Tower," he broadcast, as he shifted his gaze to hold mine, "JTL will be flying her first solo."

I was caught off guard. I later learned the surprise announcement of a student's first flight on her own is an instructor's standard practice. It's designed to deny the student enough time to work up a case of nerves. I was immediately overwhelmed with a rush of anticipation. *All right, Janine. It's time for you to take off, fly, and land this thing all by yourself!*

Bill assured me I was ready. "I'd like you to complete one circuit, then come back and pick me up. Take your time and relax. Do everything just as you've been taught, and you'll be fine. Be careful, but have fun, too!" With that, he climbed out and closed the door behind him, giving me one last confident and reassuring look.

I stole a quick glance at the empty instructor's seat and then set about preparing for the now-familiar drill of pre-takeoff checks. I drew in a deep breath, looked around to be sure the cabin was secured, and picked up my checklist: trim . . . set for takeoff . . . flaps . . . takeoff position. I progressed down the page, double-checking all settings as required. One last look about the cabin and instrument panel, another deep breath, and I was ready. Just as it was at the start of any of my ski races, my mind was clear and concentrated on the task ahead.

I taxied to the runway holding point and depressed the transceiver button to call the tower. "Juliet Tango Lima ready. Runway left," I stated in my most professional pilot voice.

"Juliet Tango Lima, line up," the instructions came back.

I confirmed there was no traffic on final approach to my runway. All clear. Rolling slowly to the centerline, I looked over to the wind sock for one last confirmation of wind direction and speed. It was light and variable. I studied my instruments; everything indicated normal.

I sat at the controls, engine idling, awaiting further clearance from the tower. Yes, I was excited and a bit nervous, but my mind was focused and I was confident. At last the controller's voice crackled through my headset, "Juliet Tango Lima, cleared for takeoff."

I moved my hand forward, advancing the throttle, and little JTL quickly picked up speed. Glancing in and out of the airplane, I monitored both centerline position and airspeed: passing forty, then fifty, then sixty knots, and finally, flying speed! I pulled back on the control column, and JTL nearly leapt off the runway, her nose pointing skyward. There was no turning back now. I was committed—and only I could determine the outcome of this flight.

Eyes straight ahead, I concentrated. There was a lot to do, and in the circuit, the process from takeoff to landing all happened in rapid succession. *Confirming climb rate: airspeed steady at eighty knots.* Now the three-hundred-feet checks needed to be completed. *Keep an eye on engine temperatures and pressures. Maintain runway heading.* And so, my mental checks progressed, as I turned left to join the crosswind leg of the standard landing pattern. *One thousand feet: level off and reduce throttle to circuit power.* I looked down and to my left to confirm that my flight track traced a neat rectangular pattern across the ground. So far, so good.

With hardly any time for the transition from departure, I turned left onto the downwind leg and began my pre-landing checks. When I came to the hatches (the doors) and harness (both seatbelts) check, I instinctively looked at the seat usually occupied by my instructor. On each previous flight, I'd await his reply to confirm that his side of the airplane was secure. This time, though, out of sheer joy and gratitude, I let out the biggest yell of my life: I was on my own and the pilot in command!

I took a moment to look at the airport spread out below me and then at Sydney's picturesque skyline in the distance. I don't know how to adequately describe being at the controls of an aircraft for one's first solo flight. This milestone moment was more than extraordinary for me. I stole another glance at the empty seat beside me. *Oh my God! I've still got to land this thing!* As I watched the aircraft in front of me navigate its way around the circuit pattern to land, I was determined to savor the moment. I knew then that no matter where my flight training would ultimately take me, there would never again be a flight quite like this first solo.

All too soon, my reverie ended. It was time to get back to work and set up for the approach. There was still a lot to do to get the airplane back safely on the runway. A knot formed in my stomach as I considered how my weak lower legs challenged my ability to operate the rudder pedals normally. I steeled myself to be ready to call on my athlete's will once I touched down. I needed to make sure I could keep the wheels tracking the centerline and operate the brakes. *God, I hope my legs hold up and that the compensating skills I've practiced will help me stop before I'm out of runway!*

As I made my final approach, I monitored my descent and confirmed I was at target airspeed. With everything set for touchdown, I crossed the runway threshold and reduced the power to idle. The wheels made a tiny squeak as they settled on the pavement, and I held the nosewheel off for a little longer as the speed decreased. Finally, I slid my feet up the rudder pedals and used all the strength in my legs to apply the brakes. As the plane slowed, I pushed the left pedal to steer clear of the runway and onto the taxiway. I had done it! *Woo-hoo!* The safety and success of my first solo assured, I allowed myself another triumphant shriek in the otherwise empty cockpit.

I taxied back to where Bill waited, relaying my intentions to the tower. The controller responded with my clearance and "Congratulations, Juliet Tango Lima!" After a slight pause, in a departure from his usual clipped professional tone, he added, "I'll give you nine out of ten for that one!"

Although at the time it struck me as a curious remark from a controller, I later learned why he'd allowed himself to make such a whimsical comment. During my first solo, John Guselli, whose father was a friend of Dad's, had been a controller in the tower. Naturally, John had taken an interest in my flying, and his bearing witness to that special flight made the event all that more meaningful to both of us.

I parked the plane, and Bill rushed up to greet me with enthusiastic congratulations. "Well done! That was a nice landing." He extended his hand for me to shake.

I smiled to myself. It was a good landing, and now I had soloed!

Back at the flight school, I was greeted with kudos. My first pilot-in-command flight was officially recorded and stamped in my logbook. With that milestone behind me, I'd at last passed my initiation into the school's team of aviators, never again to be stared at as an oddity. I was elated. This was a day I vowed never to forget. I couldn't wait to tell Mum and Dad. How proud they would be seeing their daughter defy the odds that a few months earlier were so overwhelmingly stacked against her.

From that point on, I dove into my flying even more seriously. It wasn't only because advancing my flying skills demanded focus, it was also because I had something to prove to myself and to those who thought piloting an airplane was beyond my ability. After my first solo flight, I was well on my way to my ultimate goal of becoming a licensed pilot. The progression in subsequent lessons took me back to the training area for more demanding exercises, like simulated forced landings—one of many practices I hoped I would never be called on to perform for real. I learned basic instrument flying (controlling the airplane without outside reference) and precautionary landing procedures, both prerequisites to departing the training area and landing at distant airports on cross-country flights. Around the circuit and in the training area, help via radio was always close by, but once away from the security of the airport, I'd need the knowledge and confidence to handle in-flight issues on my own.

Having logged the required instructional and solo flights after two months of additional lessons, the time came for my private pilot's license test. My examiner was the chief instructor at the school, Neville, an encouraging and supportive man who'd shown great interest in my progress since I first began my lessons. On test day, I arrived to the distressing news that the aircraft I had been flying—whose systems and operations I'd studied so diligently for my test—was out of service. I was offered an alternative. I could take the test in a more complex aircraft, one with an adjustable-pitch propeller, but doing so required systems knowledge beyond the aircraft I knew.

Here was my quandary: Do I postpone until my usual aircraft is returned to the flight line, or do I take the test as planned, albeit in a plane I'd never flown? Prepared and eager to take the test, I chose to receive some last-minute training in the more complex plane. In addition to the performance differences, there was an extra power lever (for the different propeller) to worry about managing in all phases of flight. After a couple hours learning a new set of speed and power settings—in addition to becoming familiar with the differences in the plane itself—my cram course was complete, and I presented myself for the test.

Once Neville and I had gone through the required ground preparation and reviews, I went out to the plane and did my pre-flight inspection. Neville observed. From time to time, he'd challenge me with questions about functions of critical parts of the plane, to make sure I demonstrated adequate understanding of the equipment. Finally, we settled into the cockpit, and I executed the pre-start and pre-taxi checklists.

After takeoff, I was directed to the training area for the in-flight maneuvers section of the test. Neville sat beside me, hardly saying a word. I was a little nervous but reassured myself that if I did every task as I'd been taught, I would be okay. This was no different than a World Cup ski race. I'd trained and studied for this moment, and I was ready.

When we'd reached the training area and confirmed clear traffic, Neville got down to business. Working through the examiner's checklist, he drilled me on the maneuvers I had learned in training, each requiring completion within delineated parameters of airspeed, altitude, and heading. I had to demonstrate stall proficiency (intentionally flying too slowly and then recovering); hold altitude through steep, forty-five-degree banked turns; and exhibit mastery of aircraft control in a variety of other flight regimes. The test was a series of challenges with little respite, but I kept up.

Suddenly, Neville pulled the power back to idle, to simulate an engine failure. My immediate response, as trained, was to find an open space suitable for an emergency landing—a paddock, for instance—and make the decisions and preparations I'd need to if we had really lost power. I set up an approach to a large open field, went through my off-airport landing checks, and continued my powerless glide, until Neville finally said, "Okay, go around." With relief, I added full power and raised the nose to climbing attitude, hoping the poor farmer in the house below wasn't too perturbed with our impromptu buzz.

On our way back to the airport, Neville surprised me with yet another simulated engine failure. This time, he reduced power above a built-up area that gave few suitable options for landing. I spotted a small sports field to my left. "I'm heading there," I said confidently and began my emergency drills. Satisfied, Neville again waved me off, and we returned to the airport.

Tired from the day and the stress of the test, I rallied my efforts to shine on the approach and landing phases. Once down and clear of the runway, we taxied back to the school. All the while, Neville made not so much as a peep. I stopped the plane and stared expectantly at him, my gaze reflecting the unease of not yet knowing the test outcome.

Finally, he beamed at me with a broad grin. "Congratulations, young lady! You're now the holder of a private pilot's license." He shook my hand and gave me a curt, salutary nod. About to turn blue, I exhaled, and I allowed myself to sink back into my seat in blessed relief. I had passed. *I am a licensed pilot!*

Andrew waited at the edge of the tarmac. One glimpse of my smile was enough for him to know how I had done. "I guess you passed," he said.

"Yes." I laughed. "How can you tell?"

"How about a cup of tea?" Neville asked, putting his arm around my shoulder. Like Andrew and the other instructors, Neville knew how much effort had gone into my training and the challenges I'd overcome. I could sense his pride in my accomplishment, the sincerity of his approbation.

This enormous sense of achievement was far greater than anything I had felt before—far more than winning a ski race, better than a triathlon podium finish, surpassing even the prospect of being an Olympic contender. Nearly every day since my accident, I'd felt as if life challenged me to say "Yes, I can" to every hurdle in my path to recovery.

It may not have been part of the original plan, but becoming a CAA Private Pilot was my equivalent of an Olympic Gold Medal.

After our celebratory tea, I did the thing that any newly minted private pilot would do: I booked my first flight as a pilot in command (PIC) two days hence. My first passengers would be Mum and Dad. Although my parents were delighted with my success, Mum wasn't thrilled by my proposal. Flight in a light aircraft was not on her bucket list. To assuage her concerns, I explained the long-standing aviation tradition of newly certified pilots taking their parents as first passengers. Faced with the prospect of breaking tradition, Mum relented. Dad, on the other hand, was beside himself with excitement and needed no such prodding.

The weather on the day of our flight was perfect. It was clear and sunny, which reassured Mum. We were booked to fly Juliet Tango Oscar, my trusty Tobago. After I completed the pre-flight paperwork, I escorted my passengers to the aircraft. As I'd been trained, I took this flight seriously and added an extra bit of professionalism, both to assert my standing as a PIC and to put Mum more at ease. With my parents buckled in and my pre-flight inspection checks done, I gave them the standard emergency procedures briefing. Mum showed visible chagrin as I ticked off the litany of things that could go wrong, especially upon repeatedly hearing the word "emergency"—but I assured her it was just a precaution, pointing out that the same briefing is given on an airliner.

I taxied to the run-up bay, did my engine and system checks, and lined up on the runway. With the flourish of a professional pilot (one on whose certificate the ink had barely dried), I advanced the power and sent us hurtling down the runway. As soon as we took off, Mum, who was sitting in the back, leaned forward and tapped me on the shoulder. "Janine, what's that on the wing?" I could hear the nervousness in her voice.

I looked out to the left and saw liquid—fuel—streaming out of the filler cap for the wing's petrol tank. "Oh, that's normal. Don't worry about it," I consoled her. At the moment, I didn't have a clue what might be causing the leak, though it didn't appear to be serious enough to abort the flight.

I continued toward the training area, with a close eye on the liquid pouring off the wing. To my dismay, the fuel continued siphoning overboard. At this point, prudence dictated a return to the airport to sort out the cause. I calmly advised the control tower of my intentions, landed without incident, and taxied back to the school. One of the instructors came out to see what was wrong.

It turned out to be as non-threatening as I'd guessed. The line service had overfilled the tank and excess fuel was venting itself out of the tank through a port designed for that purpose. Problem solved. Our confidence was bolstered, and we got back in the plane and took off again.

Once we were out in the training area, I flew around and showed them the sights. Dad reveled in the bird's-eye perspective and in knowing his daughter was pilot in command of his flight. I had a sneaking suspicion Mum enjoyed herself too. Emboldened, I showed Dad some of the maneuvers I'd learned. I made the unfortunate choice of reducing the power to idle to demonstrate a glide descent, which made Mum panic. She tapped me on the shoulder again, only this time with more urgency: "Don't you practice one of your so-called stalls with me in the airplane!"

"Don't worry, Mum. I'm just descending to go back to the airport," I fibbed, as I transitioned to a standard approach and a subsequent smooth landing.

Back at the school, Mum chatted with one of the instructors.

"You're brave," he said. "I *teach* flying, and my parents still won't go up with me!"

Oh no, the jig is up! I'd made up the story of the tradition, and it appeared now I'd been ratted out.

"What do you mean?" exclaimed Mum, as she turned to face me with the stern look of a parent who had uncovered a ruse. Holding my gaze and undoubtedly seeing the twinkle in my eyes, she continued, "Janine said *all* new pilots take their parents up for a flight after their test—some sort of tradition."

"Not my parents! They're still too scared, and they would never have come on my first passenger flight!"

Mum continued to glare at me, though her eyes and the corners of her mouth belied her consternation. "That's not what Janine told us." I couldn't look, but I would have bet Dad was smiling.

Despite Mum's feigned indignity at being had, it was apparent she and Dad were bursting with pride at what I had achieved. In return, I basked in their recognition, happy to share the joy of that first passenger flight with my parents and begin to repay them for the months of heartache they'd endured.

› 17 ‹

I was six months shy of my college graduation at the time of my accident. Well on the road to recovery and with encouragement from friends and professors, I decided to complete my degree in physical education. Enrolling again at University of Technology Sydney, my first stop was at the medical center to pick up a disabled driver's pass. Before my accident, I would often ride my bike to class; now, parking in the disabled spots was a constant reminder of my loss. The courses in physical education also accentuated my feelings of inadequacy, especially because the field of study naturally attracted athletes. Still another limitation imposed by my injuries: I continued my struggle with catheters, making me all the more self-conscious about my body.

The most obvious challenges to completing my degree were the limitations on my physical movement, strength, and agility. I was unable to participate in any of the practical courses because those athletic endeavors demanded more than my disabled body could deliver. Instead, I continued my rehab work and enrolled in the mandatory theory subjects in education, which allowed me some progress toward graduation by at least completing the teaching component of my degree.

I continued to fly whenever possible. In stark contrast to my time on the college campus, I felt alive and confident when airborne. Seated at the controls, in command of my plane, no one could notice that I walked funny—indeed, that I had any physical limitations whatsoever. As a pilot, I was capable, assured, and temporarily freed of the complications from my injuries.

Struggling to fit in at school in a field of study centered on the physical body, I quickly grew disillusioned with pursuing my degree. I couldn't identify any solid options for changing majors, so I quit college and decided to concentrate on advancing my flying career instead. As always, Mum and Dad were supportive of my decision. Their only concern remained my happiness and well-being.

First, I trained for an unrestricted private pilot license, or UPPL. After mastering the fundamentals of navigation, meteorology, and advanced flight rules and procedures, I could use this new rating to fly anywhere in the country, not just regionally around Bankstown.

Finding it impractical to travel to the ground school classes held in Sydney, I bought the appropriate manuals, and as before, began a rigorous home study. After a few weeks of intensive work, I took the written test and passed. With ground courses under my belt, it was time to tackle the practical side of things in flight. I discovered there would be a lot more involved in this advanced rating than in my initial licensing, not the least of which was the more detailed planning and preparation before each distance flight.

My first trip out of the training area was to be to Cessnock Airport, about one hundred miles north, where I'd land and prepare for the return to Bankstown. I was to fly under visual flight rules (VFR), which meant I'd chart my progress without electronic aids by comparing my view out the window to a detailed map.

To set my course, I employed a tried-and-true navigation technique called dead reckoning. I started out on my plotted heading, compared checkpoints to the time calculated for reaching them, and made necessary corrections to the ground track and estimated time of arrival (ETA) as needed. In addition to the demands of flying the aircraft and staying on course, I had to maintain radio contact with flight service (an inflight advisory air-traffic facility), fill in my flight plan, accommodate climbs and descents, and maneuver the aircraft to a safe approach and landing upon arrival.

I planned this first trip carefully, marked my maps with courses and checkpoints (the distance between them constituting what's known as a leg), and filled out my flight plan. The cumulative time required for each of the legs gave me the ETA at Cessnock. With pre-flight work complete, I needed two reviews of my plan: first with my instructor Andrew, who would accompany me on this first foray, and then with flight service. Once lodged and stamped, my first cross-country flight plan was approved, and we returned to the flying school to prepare for departure.

Andrew and I took off, and were soon following the light aircraft lane, a designated departure for Bankstown that assured separation from the large transport jets arriving from the north, and headed for Sydney. Instead of letting me absorb this new and challenging process, Andrew lumped everything on me at once.

"Okay, Janine, what frequency should you be on? Do you have to make any radio calls? Where does the Sydney airspace end? What about the military airspace to the west?" Andrew's flurry of questions felt like badgering, and I got a bit flustered. Once we were out of the busy Bankstown control zone, though, I regained my composure and took time to enjoy the scenery en route as I double-checked our progress. I realized later that his technique was intended to hone my ability to stay focused in the face of distractions.

We flew over the sprawling suburbs of Sydney, with their red-roofed houses and countless backyard pools. As our flight progressed, the landscape morphed from a string of bedroom communities to wineries, farms, and estates. As we neared Cessnock, I could hear on the radio that the area was buzzing with other aircraft. I'd have to be extra vigilant as we got closer; there was a large flight-training school based there.

The approach and landing proved uneventful. We took the opportunity to disembark, stretch our legs, and celebrate the success of my first cross-country flight. Then we made the return flight to home base without any problems. I was pleased that my meticulous planning for this first foray from the familiar Bankstown environment had kept us on course and on time.

After my training flight out of Bankstown's control zone, my work progressed according to the curriculum outlined for my rating. In just over a month, I had completed all my necessary navigation sorties, logging flights all across the eastern Australian countryside without once getting lost or rattled. It was time to sit for my practical exam. Unbeknownst to me at the time, this test would challenge far more than my flying ability.

Once again, Neville was my testing officer, and I understood from his briefing that there would be some added tasks during the flight to Cessnock. Andrew warned me that I would probably be asked to execute a diversion, simulating deteriorating weather. Responding to these in-flight curveballs meant doing all of the tedious calculations on the fly, literally: taking coordinates and calculating times, creating a new flight plan, and radioing flight service to inform them of the changes, all while piloting the airplane within the required heading and altitude restrictions.

Fortunately, the weather on the day of my test was picture perfect: blue skies and only a breath of wind, ideal for flying. I headed down to the briefing office to collect the en route weather details and other information I would need to plan my flight. I had less than an hour until we were due to depart, so I had to be efficient in my preparations.

Then the unthinkable happened: my stomach began to cramp. The unpredictable effects of bladder and bowel control associated with spinal cord damage meant I always tried to stay close to a bathroom. *I need to go now!* I dropped my bags in the briefing room and shuffled toward the bathroom as quickly as my weak legs could carry me. By the time I got there, the severity of the cramps had me doubled over with urgency. I flung open the cubicle door and swung around onto the toilet seat, but I was seconds too late. As I maneuvered to sit, the pressure in my abdomen released with the worst possible case of diarrhea imaginable.

Are you kidding me? Fuck! Of all possible times for this to happen, why now, with the start of my flight test just minutes away? Sitting on the seat, I buried my face in my hands and began to cry. There couldn't be a worse time for a bowel accident. Wiping my nose on my sleeve, I lifted my skirt to assess the damage, and it was way worse than I'd feared. The diarrhea was everywhere, soaking my underwear and even running down my legs. I was a mess. *Please, God, don't let anyone walk in now!*

My heart racing, I ran through a hurried list of options, the most obvious being that I couldn't imagine a better excuse to pack it in and go home. Could I somehow sneak out of the school without anyone noticing? Even if I could, how would I explain my sudden disappearance to the examiner waiting to begin my test, to my instructor, or even to my parents?

Then again, I wondered how I could possibly sit for my test in my soiled clothes and in such a dispirited state? I had to make a decision. In that moment, a wave of resolve and determination swept over me. I had come too far and worked too hard to give in to this indignity. I would not let this accident threaten my future as a pilot.

Sizing up my situation, I realized I had the rudiments of a solution at hand: toilet paper, soap, and a hand dryer were all available in the bathroom. I pulled off my underwear and skirt, unrolled reams of toilet paper, and methodically began to clean. Every so often, I peered out of the cubicle door to check for anyone else in the bathroom, but the coast remained clear. Thank goodness! Once I'd cleaned my body, I threw my clothes in the sink and turned on the tap until everything was soaked. Lathering them in hand soap, I began scrubbing.

Clothed only in my shirt, I kept glancing over my shoulder at the door, praying no one would walk in. What a sight that would be: me, naked from the waist down, scrubbing my undies in the sink. Imagining what I might say in such an awkward encounter, I managed a bit of humor in my internal dialogue as I continued to clean: *Um . . . my washing machine at home is broken. Thought I'd catch up on some laundry while I was preparing for my pilot test!*

Once my clothes were washed and rinsed, I held them under the hand dryer on the wall. I glanced at my watch: only forty minutes until test time. *I can't wait any longer. This will have to do.* I put my clothes back on. They were still damp against my skin.

I opened the door and peered out. Seeing no one nearby, I darted, as best I could, down the hall in an attempt to make a quick exit to the car to complete the last piece of my plan. To my horror, Neville, my examiner, appeared from behind the desk.

"Hey, Shepherd. You almost ready to start the test?"

"Um . . . ah . . . yep . . . almost ready. Just left something in the car. Back soon!" I said, as I dashed out the door, limped to my car, and sped away.

Managing the one-hour trip home was out of the question, so instead I drove like a maniac to the nearest drugstore. I purchased diarrhea medicine and swallowed a double dose on the spot. I bought some deodorant as well. With a few squirts of that, my recovery plan was complete—with hardly a minute to spare.

I drove across the airport to the briefing office to file my flight plan with the authorities, then made my way to the school. I grabbed my headsets and my flight bag and headed down to the tarmac to begin pre-flighting the aircraft. I was a bit rattled, but the tremendous relief of having sidestepped my bodily crisis helped me calm down and shift my thoughts to the tasks at hand.

The entire time I prepared for the upcoming three-hour flight test, I harbored a fear that the diarrheal medication might not take effect in time, if at all. I froze for an instant with an unimaginable thought: *What if I had a recurrence in the airplane?* That would be a disaster. I was about to spend the next three hours trapped in a small cockpit with someone I barely knew, not to mention that he held my pilot rating in his hands. To quiet these fearful thoughts, I reminded myself that, after all, it was just a body. I had to face the fact that some parts of it were, indeed, broken. Yes, it would be embarrassing if I had another accident, but I would deal with it. I wanted my advanced rating so badly and had worked too hard for it to let the threat of another accident stop me now.

The day didn't improve much after its inauspicious start. The flight test was grueling and, as expected, Neville threw every imaginable challenge my way. He ordered me to divert to a different airport than I had planned and then restricted my view to the panel only, to simulate instrument flying conditions in foul weather. To top off the hazing, he directed me to land at Sydney's busy (international) Mascot Airport, a small-airplane pilot's nightmare. All the while, in the back of my mind, I prayed that my disgruntled stomach would hang on long enough to get me on the ground without further incident.

With all the in-flight trials completed, Neville directed me to return to base at Bankstown Airport. I now knew I was going to make it through both tests: flying and bodily functions. We landed uneventfully and taxied back to the school. As before, Neville sat stone-faced. I shut down the engine, closed out my checklist, and then turned to Neville to receive his verdict.

"Congratulations, Shepherd," he said enthusiastically. "You passed!"

I smiled and shook the hand he offered.

"You are now a full-fledged unrestricted private pilot," he said and added for emphasis, "Fly anywhere you want now."

As Neville walked back to the school, I put my head back, took a deep breath, and closed my eyes. "Thank you," I whispered. Relief and gratitude washed over me.

› 18 ‹

I've often been asked how I could afford to pay for my flying courses. Like so many aspiring aviators, I managed a pay-as-you-go program and creatively cobbled together funds from various sources. Over the years, I'd been able to stash away some savings from odd jobs I'd held throughout my schooling, from waitressing to aerobics instruction. My parents loaned me some money, as did a local bank. The balance came from unused funds left over from a scholarship I was granted before my accident. At that time, flight training was far less expensive than it is today. Then, as now, budding pilots tend to apply themselves fully to each rung of the aviation ladder, often scrounging nickels and dimes to pay for lessons and study materials. I did the same.

The progression through flight certification requires a pilot to gain experience, study, and take a practical exam for each added level of permissions. Now that I had my unrestricted private pilot certification, the next qualification in sequence would normally be a commercial pilot's license, or CPL, a requisite to fly charter, scenic tours, and similar paid operations. I hadn't given any thought to this rating. A CPL was necessary only for pilots planning a career in aviation, which was the furthest thing from my mind. I still couldn't walk properly. Who in their right mind would hire me as a professional pilot?

Taking into account these and other considerations, I decided instead to get my license endorsed for another plane in the flying-school fleet: the Trinidad. It was equipped with a more powerful engine, a controllable propeller, and a retractable undercarriage. This meant learning how to manage these more complex systems, and for that, Neville himself would take me through both the training and the subsequent check ride for the endorsement.

As I wound down my Trinidad training, Neville and I were enjoying our now-customary postflight tea and chat when he paused thoughtfully and changed the subject with a surprising suggestion.

"Shepo," he said, using his nickname for me, "now that you've got your unrestricted PPL, why don't you think about getting your CPL?"

"My commercial rating? Neville, are you kidding? To start, who would ever give me a job?"

"I would," he said without hesitation, looking me straight in the eye. I returned his stare, but he didn't flinch. Apparently, he wasn't joking.

"What sort of job?" I pressed him further.

"Well, if you get your commercial license and then your instructor's rating, I'd hire you to teach."

I was floored. "Are you serious, Neville? You'd give me a job *teaching* flying?"

"You bet. Think about it, and let me know."

I drove home consumed with thoughts of Neville's offer. He wanted me to consider training to be not just a qualified commercial pilot but also an instructor. I swelled with pride at the thought that Neville held my skills and abilities in such high regard. I'd managed to come such a long way in a short period of time. Then my mental pendulum swung the other way when I imagined my students seeing me limp down to the aircraft to teach them how to fly. *Don't worry,* I imagined reassuring them. *It's just that I was run over by a truck. I can't feel my legs. I'm a partial paraplegic. But you're in safe hands—lightning never strikes twice!*

As I ruminated, I realized that advancing as far as flight instructor came down to one daunting crux: I had to pass the more stringent CPL medical examination. I thought back to my PPL exam and my physician and ally, Dr. Henderson; maybe I could enlist his support. I had nothing to lose, so I decided to take Neville up on his suggestion and at least give it a go.

The next day I made an appointment to see Dr. Henderson. Not surprisingly, he remembered me—not many of his flight applicants sport a body brace. He was happy to see me more mobile and offered enthusiastic praise when I told him I had qualified as an unrestricted private pilot. It was then I decided to go for broke. "So, I've come for my commercial pilot's license medical exam," I stated with confidence.

He stared at me for a moment. Then, he took off his glasses, wiped them on his shirt, and replaced them on his nose. "Janine," he said, in his wavering voice, "I think it's fantastic that you've decided to do this." He paused for a moment. "But a CPL—and the responsibility that goes with it—is something entirely different from flying for pleasure. We're talking about other people's lives, not just yours."

My heart and hopes sank.

"You see, with your complicated medical history . . . well, I don't imagine the CAA has ever had an applicant with the extent of your injuries. Not only will I need to confirm you're one hundred percent fit and up to CPL standards, but the CAA will scrutinize every detail of your application," he cautioned. Then, perceiving my intent to give it a go regardless of the odds, he sighed and said, "So, we had best get started. We'll have to do a thorough job, and it may take a while."

Dr. Henderson was going to give me a chance! I understood why he was taking it so seriously: once he had recommended me as qualified to hold the license, he could be held accountable if something went wrong on one of my commercial flights because of medical reasons. This liability aside, I was confident he would do everything he could within the required standards to pass me. He wanted to help me and believed I could handle the challenge if given the opportunity.

So I was not surprised that the CPL examination took a lot longer than the previous one. Some of my reflexes were still missing, and I had discernible weakness in both my legs and feet. I couldn't stand on my toes, and I walked slowly, with a noticeable limp. My balance wasn't good, half my body was numb, and I was marked from head to toe with scars. My spine was held together by a prominent rib patch, and I suffered from bladder and bowel dysfunction. With such a list of medical shortcomings, I didn't come close to the ideal picture of a commercial pilot!

After an exhaustive review, Dr. Henderson recommended me for the CPL license, adding his best wishes for my new career. As before, I still had to get the go-ahead from the CAA, but that was out of my hands. For the time being, I'd made it past the first hurdle to becoming a commercial pilot.

The next step toward my CPL required me to log additional hours of flying without an instructor aboard, building time as a PIC, or pilot in command. One creative way to accomplish that, I reckoned, was to plan a trip to central Australia's outback, enlisting a few of my friends as passengers. I had no trouble lining up volunteers. The idea of a holiday that covered half the continent, made readily accessible by a small airplane, was enticement enough.

Two of my girlfriends signed on immediately: Meredith, a former schoolmate who'd become a lawyer, and Linda, a flight attendant. The third passenger was an American we'd crossed paths with while he was on holiday in Australia. We called him Dude, a reflection of his amusing habit of addressing nearly everyone else by that moniker.

Our plan was to fly across the desert to the iconic sandstone monolith in the heart of Australia, Ayers Rock, otherwise known as Uluru, the official aboriginal name. We would travel via Broken Hill, the country's longest-running mining town, and then back across Queensland and down to Dubbo. I spent hours working out the logistics of the flight and making arrangements for each of our stops and layovers. In addition to maps and other navigation items, I planned to carry a first-aid kit and plenty of water. We'd be flying over some harsh and barren country, much of it desert, so I was careful to cover all contingencies.

We gathered at the airport on the morning of the flight and loaded our gear into Juliet Tango Yankee, the Trinidad. I'd already checked the weather, filed my flight plan, and done a thorough inspection of the plane. My passengers were excited, especially the Dude, a happy-go-lucky "Yank," keen for an outback adventure.

We hopscotched from one outpost to the next, stopping mainly to stretch our legs, take a bathroom break, and top off our fuel. Our final stop was in the tiny settlement of Leigh Creek, in eastern central South Australia, where we spent the first night. Hoping to make some time in the cool morning air, we struck out the next morning at dawn, but it wasn't long before we encountered turbulent, stifling conditions from the intense heat of the desert below. Soon, perspiration began to stream down my forehead, making it almost impossible to keep my headsets from sliding off in the bumpy air. For hours on end and in all directions, there was nothing but sand stretching to every horizon. Without the benefit of distinct landmarks, I had to concentrate on holding an exact heading until I could confirm our position, lest we ended up lost over a forbidding and hostile desert.

My unrelenting attention to cross-checking our position rewarded us with a safe landing at a remote outback strip called Oodnadatta. This was but a small town, surrounded by vast cattle ranches, many of them larger than some European countries. There we refueled and set off on the final leg of our outbound journey. We'd been in the air for over five hours and were drained from the heat and relentless turbulence when I spotted the distinctive silhouette of Ayers Rock. Majestically jutting out of the otherwise unremarkable desert ahead, it was an unmistakable and magnificent landmark. I felt a tremendous sense of relief. We'd done it!

The heat rising off the desert floor made for a bumpy approach and landing, so all of us were happy when JTY touched down safely at Yulara, the resort airport closest to the Rock itself. As we taxied in, I could take a well-earned mental break and allow myself a moment of self-reflection: I had flown all the way from Sydney to the heart of Australia with nobody to assist me. Now it was time to relax, enjoy myself, and recover a bit from the stress.

We spent an exciting few days exploring the Rock and its surroundings. We were all keen to climb it, including me, although I didn't yet know how I would manage with my wobbly legs. When we began our ascent, I was discouraged to find that the start of the climb was nearly vertical. Using the rope strung along the path to aid in scaling the incline, we set off as a team. The steep grade helped me make a crucial if somewhat humbling discovery: I could climb, so long as it was on all fours. No matter that it looked odd to the casual observer, I happily crawled, eager to reach the summit along with my friends.

Atop the giant red rock, the four of us celebrated with a glass of champagne, courtesy of the Dude. In addition to the by-now tepid refreshment, our reward for this strenuous climb was the breathtaking view: endless horizons and red dirt stretching as far as the eye could see. Mesmerized by the varying shades of color in the landscape, we stayed there until the heat of the day overcame us, at which point we made our way back down.

All too soon, our stay at Uluru came to an end, and we set off on our return journey. Linda had flown by airline back to Sydney for work, so now it was just Meredith, the Dude, and me. Our flight progressed without incident until late in the day, when flight service radioed to warn us of developing thunderstorms expected at our next stop. Their advice was to divert to a safer alternate for the night. Just as I'd trained—and done for Neville in simulation on my exam flight—I took out my maps to determine Plan B.

We'd already been airborne for hours over an unremarkable desert landscape that provided scant opportunity to reliably fix our position. In addition to the threat of this real-life diversion, I sensed with growing uneasiness that we might have drifted off course. My map indicated that there should have been a small airstrip in our vicinity, but I couldn't see anything remotely resembling a runway—only a vast and unbroken expanse of sand and rock.

Weighing the time we'd been aloft against our remaining fuel, I couldn't afford the risk of hunting for an airstrip that I might never find. Taking a moment to regain my composure, I studied my map, only this time I searched for the nearest place with an instrument aid, a radio transmitter used to help pilots navigate that is called an NDB, or non-directional beacon. Using an NDB would allow me to enlist the aircraft's instruments to identify the direction to the source of the signal and, thus, the airport from which it was being broadcast. The airport beacon I identified was an outpost I'd never heard of, Windorah. Tuning my instrument receiver to confirm the correct radio frequency, I called flight service and advised them of our intent to land there.

With the unplanned diversion, by the time we reached the vicinity of Windorah, we'd be into the last of our daylight, as well as our fuel, save reserves. Since I wasn't night-flight certified, I was keen to find that landing strip and get on the ground as soon as possible. I enlisted Dude's aid as a spotter, and we were all relieved to see the faint outline of a runway in the desert below. I circled the airport and prepared to land. By the time I touched down, there was a fuel truck waiting for us. As soon as I parked the aircraft and shut down the engine, the Dude jumped out and, with a touch of drama, kissed the ground.

"Gawd, it's good to be here!" he declared in his characteristic drawl.

I couldn't have agreed more. All told, we had been in the air for more than five hours, flying over forbidding terrain with few options for landing. I was glad to be on terra firma myself.

I looked up to see an imposing figure striding toward the aircraft. I was surprised to discover it was a woman—a big one at that.

"G'day," she said, in a voice deep enough for any man. "Guess youse'd be wantin' some fuel?"

"Yes, that's right," I replied, deferentially. Judging from her looks, I didn't want to get on her wrong side.

"What sort of plane is this anyway?" she growled.

"Oh, it's called a Trinidad."

"I'll just call it shit for short," she said dismissively.

Fine, I thought, *just give us the fuel.*

After refueling, she instructed us to follow her to a tiny shed tucked away at the side of the strip. On the wall outside was a sign announcing "WINDORAH," with the D painted backward. What sort of town were we about to spend the night in?

"Guess youse'd be wantin' some dinner, too," the woman said, as she handed me a receipt.

"Yes, that would be great," I answered. "And somewhere to spend the night."

She got on the phone—the old-fashioned wind-up kind you'd expect to find hanging on the wall in a turn-of-the-century saloon—and cranked it enthusiastically.

"Yeah, that's right, I got 'em. They'll be coming in for dinner," she said to the person on the other end. I stole a glance at my passengers. None of us was sure what she'd meant by "got 'em," but most certainly we were committed to her charge.

I decided it might break the ice to offer introductions. "Anyway, my name is Janine, and this is Meredith, and this is the Dude," I said, holding my hand out.

Her outsized paw almost crushed my hand. "You can call me Bub," and looking straight at Dude, she added, "I'll just call you Shithead." She roared with laughter at her own joke.

I stole a glance at Meredith and saw that she was as puzzled as I, but when I turned to the Dude, he was grinning. "This is fantastic. She's great," he offered, with an enthusiasm that suggested he was game for whatever adventure Windorah had in store for us.

Bub escorted us to our transport into town, a beat-up truck parked beyond the strip. Attempting to follow her giant stride over a low barbed-wire fence, I instead got my jeans caught and fell flat on my face.

Bub offered me a hand up. "Hey, that was a good one!" she said with a good-natured laugh.

Once on our way, my two passengers and I immediately exchanged fearful glances. Bub drove much too fast for our comfort, and the short ride into town was proving riskier than our five-hour flight. But Bub delivered us without a scratch to the local pub, where we found the entire population of Windorah had gathered to greet us—all six of them!

Bub brandished a ham of a fist at the men seated at the bar and snarled, "I got 'em. They're mine!" I had no idea what she meant by that, but apparently she'd assumed the role of protector as well as host.

Looking at the ragtag group from Windorah, I was struck by their appearance: everyone in the bar was filthy, covered head to toe in the area's red dirt. The notable exception was the barman. This was a relief because he was the one responsible for getting our dinner.

By now, my crew and I were famished, so any food was welcomed. We were surprised by a genuine home-cooked dinner, and we eagerly devoured every scrap.

As we finished the last few bites, one of the barflies, an elderly man, approached us unsteadily. "G'day," he said in a drunken slur. "Where's the pilot?" He had to hold on to the bar to keep from falling over.

"Me, I'm the pilot," I replied.

"Go on!" he hiccupped. "I always wanted to fly. Can you teach me?"

I wasn't sure quite how to brush him off, but I wanted to do so as politely as possible. I didn't want to offend my hosts, but I reckoned he wasn't pilot material. He seemed barely capable of managing his drink, let alone flying a plane. Finally, one of his mates, who'd decided enough was enough, came over to rescue me.

"Don't take any notice of him," he interrupted. "His name is Sandy Kidd, and he's pulling your leg. This old man has more flying hours under his belt than you can poke a stick at—about twenty thousand hours at the last count."

Well, didn't I feel like a fool, writing off a pilot as seasoned as Sandy as unfit, while I sat smugly with all of a hundred hours to my name! I looked over at the Dude for some solace at my gaffe, only to find him cornered by an elderly woman as inebriated as the men.

"G'day, me name's Margie," I heard her say. "Hey, do you know any songs?" She took another swig from her beer, half of it ending up on the floor.

Windorah may have been a small village, but we were finding it was chockablock with salty characters. They were harmless and welcoming, though, so we spent the rest of the night chatting up these colorful locals, playing darts, and enjoying a beer with them.

When we headed off next morning, I circled Sandy's nearby property, curious to see it after talking aviation with such an interesting fellow. I was surprised to see an airstrip in pristine condition and a couple of large hangars beside it as well. Given how sensitive I'd become to being judged for my physical limitations, I felt a pang of remorse for how I behaved upon meeting Sandy and taking him at face value.

When we made it to our originally planned destination of Charleville later in the day, I happened to mention our stay in Windorah to the blokes in the briefing office.

"Oh, so you flew over Little Dell. That's Sandy Kidd's property," one of them said. I was surprised that he'd heard of the crusty, old, back-country pilot. My curiosity aroused, I pressed for more information and learned that Sandy Kidd was a bit of a legend in this section of outback. One of the most experienced pilots in Australia, he was also known as a humanitarian who had been decorated by the Queen. Whenever and wherever the need, it was often Sandy to the rescue. His piloting skills and experience were held in such high regard, they told me, that whenever he flew to the nearest large city airport, at Brisbane, he didn't have to bother to get clearance like everyone else.

Instead, he'd radio flight service and say, "It's Sandy Kidd," and the controllers would always make way for his arrival.

More than serving to hone my flying skills, that special air tour with my friends taught me a valuable lesson about humanity. It's important to remain open-minded and not to judge based solely on appearances. That's a theme I would return to repeatedly in my life, and a courtesy I hoped others would grant me as well.

› 19 ‹

I was approaching the two-year deadline the doctors had given me for my spinal cord to heal, the point in time that would reveal the final extent of regained function. To date, I hadn't seen evidence of the nerve regrowth I had hoped for. Functions I assumed would be forthcoming had yet to manifest, like sensation in the lower part of my body, stronger muscles, and bladder and bowel improvement. I now faced the increasing likelihood that some limitations would be with me for life.

To consider this was a blow to both my optimism and my determination to defy the odds I'd been given. I had invested so much time and effort in rehabilitation, assuming that my mobility would improve, that I hadn't yet come to terms with what now seemed inevitable. As difficult and heartbreaking as it was to accept, I had to cut the few remaining ties to my old life, including my social circle of athlete friends and my aspiration to represent Australia as an Olympic ski racer. I had to fully embrace a new persona, one that took into account my disabilities.

Perhaps the most painful decision to come out of this shift was to end my relationship with Daven, my boyfriend of five years. I was concerned that he would never really understand the struggle I would face in a physical relationship that would certainly be altered by my disabilities. I was fragile and vulnerable with this delicate aspect of my new life and felt it best to face the future on my own.

Flying was the natural choice for a new direction in my life. On any given day, once rehab was done, I could be found at the school, logging the hours I needed to sit for my commercial license. I began to study for my Instrument Flying Rating (IFR), a certification that would allow me to navigate all but the worst weather conditions, at any time of day. I also began my IFR flight training in a twin-engine plane, so that I could receive a "multi-engine endorsement" as well.

Follow-up corrective surgeries periodically interrupted my training. The bones in my toes were shaved down so I could wear normal shoes, and the tendons in my toes were also cut to address the curling. Torn tendons in my right knee were repaired, and a plate was inserted to hold in place the broken arm bone that had not fully healed—discovered by X-ray only after I'd prodded doctors to explain the pain that persisted after the accident.

Last in this series of surgical repairs was transferring some tendons in my legs to my feet, in the hope that this might improve my gait. Weeks into recovery, with my leg immobilized in plaster, I was still on crutches and impatient to get back to flying. When the time came to remove the cast, I was surprised at the number of incisions that had been made. Dr. Stephen cautioned me to take it easy for a few weeks to ensure the healing of the tendon transfer. He recommended that I let pain be my guide and cautioned me to back off when the discomfort of bearing my weight became too much.

Dismissing his concerns as excessively conservative, I swung my leg over the side of the examining bed to test my ability to walk, but the moment my foot touched the floor, I recoiled in excruciating pain. I realized I had better keep my crutches at hand. It would be more than two weeks later before I could tolerate even so much as touching my foot to the ground. Once I progressed to my first tentative steps, my foot remained so tender that I remained hobbled.

I couldn't return to the airport for several weeks after the cast came off, so I had a lot of catching up to do. All told, that surgery had cost me more than three months of flying, and I feared I might have gotten rusty in both knowledge and airmanship. I thought it prudent to ease back in with some basic refresher flights and was relieved to find that I had retained most of my training and skills. Being immobile had made me feel like a bird whose wings had been clipped, so it felt wonderful to be both out of my cast and back in the air. Once I was confident my flying was up to scratch, I booked my exams for both the night and commercial licenses.

Passing the night flying test was a breeze. Just a week later I booked with Neville to sit for my commercial test, and that exam was a different matter entirely. It took more than four hours, by the end of which I was spent. Neville put me through the paces to assess whether both my airmanship and knowledge were up to commercial standards, so I was pleased to have handled the pressure—and to have passed.

Neville had been right all along: I could, indeed, do it. Encouraged to stay the course he had recommended, in a week's time I was due to begin my instructor's rating program. The sooner I was certified to teach, the sooner I could start working with my own cadre of students and be paid for my flight time.

The flying bug had truly bitten me. I was happiest whenever I was at the airport, happier still when aloft. My dizzying progression from my inaugural trial flights to studying for my flight-instructor rating was wondrous, exciting, and at times overwhelming. I started my instructor-rating course as the only female in a class with four male aspirants, a ratio that wasn't unusual. Aviation was still a man's world, though that didn't faze me. As an athlete, I had always trained with the guys, often as the only girl—and a competitive one at that. So in many ways, the male-dominated airport environment was something I was used to, and just as I had in my racing days, I thrived.

Each in-flight session began with Neville's briefing. He explained the exercises we would do according to the specific lesson plan. Once aloft, we would then fly dual, which meant two trainees piloted together, as one played the role of instructor and the other the student. This gave us the chance to practice teaching as well as maneuvering the airplane from the instructor's seat, both skills new to us.

After weeks of study, classroom sessions, and in-flight lessons, the day for my instructor's test arrived. All of the ratings examinations to date had been with Neville, but sitting for the instructor rating required an official Civil Aviation Authority examiner. I was the first applicant in our class to complete the flying program, so I was the first in line for the practical. None of us had any idea what to expect from this particular gentleman's testing protocol.

A former air force pilot, the CAA examiner was a serious-looking man, short with a receding hairline. In the test briefing, he instructed me to prepare particular lesson plans that I would present to him in his role-play as student. He was a man of few words, offering the barest outline of instructions. Although I'd come into the test confident in my abilities, his standoffishness made me nervous—something I suspected he cultivated. Without commenting on my performance or tipping his hand to the outcome of the first part of my practical, he advanced me from the classroom trials to the in-flight test. The examiner watched me like a hawk while I did my pre-flight on the plane. He quizzed me on the tiniest details of the aircraft and its systems, apparently with no intention of cutting me any slack.

Heeding Neville's counsel, I committed to treating my examiner as if he were a real student, which was the point of conducting the test as a role-play. Once we were airborne, I went through the lesson plan, just as I had practiced with my classmates. The examiner played his part well. He queried me on every aspect of the procedures, requiring me to explain each to him as if for a student's first time. We covered virtually every lesson in the private pilot syllabus, after which we headed over to the nearby Camden Aerodrome to shoot some circuits.

The relentless grilling and pressure notwithstanding, I held my own, flying and teaching well. As an instructor candidate, I was required to demonstrate proficiency in airmanship and knowledge while overseeing his actions as mock student. All of this had to happen with me in the right seat, which meant that the hand movements and points of reference I learned as a PIC were now reversed.

Finally, the examiner directed me to fly back to Bankstown, but not before several simulated engine failures, intended to test my forced-landing procedure over densely populated areas. Each time I needed a suitable place to put the aircraft down, there it was, the perfect spot to land had the exercise not been a simulation.

After more than two hours in the air, we finally landed and taxied back to the flying school. I was eager to get my results, but the examiner maintained his reticence even as we walked across the tarmac to the classroom. I was on tenterhooks, wondering if I'd messed up at some point. The suspense was overwhelming.

Inside the school, there was still no word, so I broke the ice and asked, "Er . . . John, would you like a cup of coffee?"

"Yes, okay," he answered flatly. He certainly was holding his cards close to his vest.

I returned from the kitchen with his coffee, and we headed off to a private room for the required debrief. He was too quiet, and I was worried. We sat down, and he looked at me for an uncomfortably long time without speaking.

"How do you think you did?" he finally asked.

"Well, I was pleased with the way I flew," I offered.

He stared at me by way of reply.

Spit it out, for goodness sake!

"Okay. Well, I'm going to pass you," he finally said. And with that, he finished his coffee, wished me luck, filled out the official paperwork, and went on his way.

And so, on June 9, 1988, a few days past the two-year anniversary of my accident, the Civil Aviation Authority bestowed on me the rating of Certificated Flight Instructor.

> 20 <

Making good on his promise, Neville hired me to teach at the Australian Flying Training School. Most of the other instructors were young career pilots, working at a flight school for only as long as it took to log the experience an airline would require for hiring. Teaching for them was a means to an end. Not so for me. I was excited to be part of the teaching cadre. Becoming an instructor meant I'd have a chance to help others achieve their dreams of flying. I embraced my job with an enthusiasm bordering on evangelical. Added to that was the tremendous feeling of accomplishment I felt attaining my instructor's rating in the face of so many challenges. Most of all, I was thrilled just to be flying, regardless of which seat I occupied.

When I wasn't teaching, the airport environment continued to be an interesting place to spend my time and observe the goings-on. One day, while I was standing out on the tarmac, a little black plane sped along the taxiway toward the run-up bay. I recognized it as one of the fleet of Robin Aircraft operated by the Sydney Aerobatic School (SAS), located across the field. With a bubble canopy offering unrestricted views and the sleek lines of its airframe, that Robin caught my eye as well as my interest.

As it taxied by, I noticed that the right-seater wasn't wearing the standard-issue white pilot shirt with epaulets, the uniform common to all instructors on the aerodrome. I recalled the oft-repeated Bankstown opinion that the instructors at SAS were a bunch of louts, not ones to toe the line of pilot protocol. Airport scuttlebutt was that they were undisciplined, taxied too fast, flew like maniacs, and placed their skills above everyone else's. The school itself was considered a hotbed of anarchism, a place where renegade aviators did pretty much as they pleased. I'd always been cautioned to give those little black Robins a wide berth when operating in the training area.

Ever the iconoclast, I was intrigued by that Robin and the school that operated it.

The thought of aerobatics—maneuvering the aircraft in unusual, eye-catching, and playful ways—fascinated me. I recalled from my instructor's course the recommendation that a few hours spent learning aerobatics would not only be great fun but also a boon to my skills. The thought of flying upside down appealed to me. Ever since I first watched an SAS aircraft tumble about doing tricks, I vowed to inquire about getting some instruction in "unusual attitudes."

The desire to try it notwithstanding, aerobatics lessons were a luxury I could hardly afford. The way I saw it, though, there was no harm in going over to the school to see what it was all about. There was something about seeing that Robin taxi past, with its swashbuckling instructor draped in the right seat, that finally prompted me to take the plunge.

The Sydney Aerobatic School was situated in a small nondescript house, not far from Bankstown Airport's main entry gate. Some of the inside walls had been knocked out to fashion a makeshift office, while the ones remaining were decorated with pictures of high-performance aircraft captured in various stages of in-flight acrobatics. The vibe was edgy and exciting. It all made aerobatics look like fun.

A friendly woman named Virginia greeted me at the front desk.

"I would like some information on learning aerobatics," I said, with the air of a pilot.

"Right. What experience do you have?"

"Well, I'm an instructor at AFTS."

"Oh, I see," she replied, as I sensed her stiffening a bit. "Have you done any aerobatics before?"

I told her I hadn't, but that I was keen to try.

"Right, well, what you'd be looking at is the phase-one aerobatics course. Here's some information on what that introductory program covers and an idea of the cost."

She explained that there were four instructors, including her husband, Noel, a former Air Force pilot and the owner of the school. Noel supervised the instructors and taught advanced aerobatics, so it would be one of the other three who would take me through the phase-one syllabus.

It wasn't yet clear how long it would be until I could afford to commit to the aerobatics course, but I knew it was only a matter of when, not if. What I didn't know was that stopping in to inquire about lessons at that ramshackle school would change the course of my aviation career, and my life.

The months went by as I continued my work as a flight instructor. When I wasn't teaching, I staffed the front desk, acting as an aviation ambassador to potential students. On one particularly quiet day, I gave the aerobatics school a follow-up call since I'd saved enough money to pay for the first lessons. I recognized the voice on the other end of the line as Virginia's, and she likewise remembered me. We exchanged pleasantries. She asked how my work was going at the school, to which I replied that it had been quiet as of late. We ended the conversation with my promise to drop over in the next few weeks to schedule a flight with one of her instructors.

Given the way we'd ended that call, it was with some measure of surprise that I arrived home that afternoon to find an intriguing message on my answering machine: "Hello, Janine, this is Virginia from SAS. I was wondering if you would drop over to the school tomorrow. I have something I would like to discuss with you. Hope to see you. Bye." I played the message again, wondering why she had called me so soon after we'd spoken. "Something to discuss." What could she want?

I arrived at work as usual at eight o'clock, but by mid-morning my curiosity was getting the better of me. During my first break from teaching, I drove across the airport to see what the cryptic phone message was about. I found Virginia and Noel in the office.

"Janine, you're probably wondering why we asked you to come see us," Virginia started. "We've been thinking of adding another instructor for a while, and we think you'd be just right. Noel and I would like to offer you a job."

I was caught completely off-guard, speechless. My surprise evident from both my expression and silence, Virginia continued to explain what they had in mind.

"Of course, you will need an aerobatics endorsement first," she noted. "Then we would have to teach you how to perform aerobatics from an instructor's point of view. Here's what we would like to offer . . ." Their plan was for me to start work behind the desk, and whenever Noel had spare time, he would train me until I was qualified to teach aerobatics.

What a surprising and delightful turn of events: from a plan to cobble together funds for the occasional lesson, I'd catapulted onto the fast track of becoming an aerobatics instructor! It was dizzying to contemplate, especially since I'd yet to do even the most basic aerobatic maneuver. But there was no beating around the bush with Virginia and Noel. After discussing a few more details, they asked me when I would be able to start. I promised Virginia and Noel I would discuss the proposal with my current employer, Neville, and get back to them.

My thoughts spun. Though I was flattered that they had offered me a job, I also harbored a tinge of suspicion. After all, I didn't see how they could know anything about me, my ability to teach, or even my skills as a pilot. It was only later that Virginia came forth with the full story.

Upon learning that I was an instructor and keen to take up aerobatics, they did a bit of snooping. Noel rang one of his old air force buddies, an aviation examiner, to see if he had heard of me. As luck would have it, Noel's buddy was none other than John, the taciturn CAA examiner who tested me for my instructor's rating. He gave me rave reviews, lauding my skills as both an aviator and an instructor. John's endorsement sealed the deal.

I decided to accept their offer, though I had a few concerns. To begin with, I could see that attaining the required endorsements would be a new level of challenge to my physical abilities. To fly aerobatics demanded extensive and quick use of the rudder as part of most maneuvers, and working those pedals with my compromised ankles and feet wasn't my strong point. What strength I'd managed to generate from my wasted legs got me through straight and level flight, but to perform aerobatics—let alone teach them—would demand much more ability. G-forces (the gravitational pull of acceleration) in abrupt maneuvers would place additional strain on my body during aerobatic flight. I wasn't sure how I'd hold up but figured I'd find a way to make it work, just as I had when first learning to fly. I had to give this unique opportunity a go, no matter what.

With Neville's blessing, I finished up my engagement at the Australian Flying Training School and turned up at SAS for the first day at my new job. Right from the start I realized it was going to be different—quite a bit so—from the teaching environment I'd been accustomed to.

One of the instructors, Tim, laughed good-naturedly when he saw me. "What's that you're wearing?" he bellowed. "You look like an instructor."

"Um, I thought this is what I was meant to wear," I said, glancing down at my pilot's uniform of blue pants and a white shirt.

"Well, that's not allowed here," Tim stated with authority. "Strictly jeans and T-shirts for us."

"Oh, well, I'll remember that tomorrow."

Noel chimed in, reassuring me with a chuckle. "Tim's right, Janine. We want people who can fly, not ones who just look like they can."

He explained that there was more to their dress code than image. Aerobatic flight required pilots to be as comfortable as possible: loose-fitting clothes and boots were the best options. A necktie was out of the question, unless you fancied a face covered by it when you turned the aircraft upside down!

Virginia helped me get oriented to the building and gave me a copy of the training syllabus to begin my studies. Even the shorthand descriptions of aerobatic maneuvers were different from anything I had seen before, as far afield as imaginable from my basic instructor's notes. Noel had patterned his syllabus on the Royal Australian Air Force curriculum, offering his clients a style of training that could pass military muster.

My first morning at SAS was consumed with paperwork and introductions to the students. I learned that aerobatics instructors encouraged a relaxed atmosphere, unlike the regimen of the typical flight-school environment. There was even a lounge where students could relax and watch TV or take their pick from an assortment of aviation videos on hand. SAS was more like being at home than at school, which likely contributed to its renegade reputation.

During my first week, I met one of the regular visitors to SAS, whom everyone called Boggie. Boggie—an abbreviation of Bograt, the nickname bestowed on the most junior officer in the Royal Australian

Air Force—was an FA-18 Hornet pilot, the youngest RAAF pilot ever selected for that fighter program. Thin as a weed and dressed in scruffy jeans and old running shoes with the odd hole in them, he gave the appearance of barely being out of school, let alone capable of commanding a sophisticated military jet. But it wasn't long before the standing behind Boggie's legendary status as a pilot became evident.

"So, how do you like aerobatics, ma'am?" he asked me, politely.

Ma'am—how charming and military proper!

"Well, I can't say. I haven't done any yet."

"You're kidding!" he exclaimed. "We'd better fix that. Let's go out and turn an airplane upside down, shall we?"

"That would be great," I said, with growing excitement.

He examined the booking sheet for the aircraft. "We'll take Sexy. No one is flying her at the moment."

Pilot humor, it seemed, had predictably twisted the registration letters "SXY" into a more edgy nickname.

Boggie escorted me to the parking area where Sexy was tied down. The sleek, black aircraft did her playful moniker justice. We did the requisite pre-flight walk-around inspection and then settled into the cockpit. I was instantly aware of the unique nature of this aircraft. Even the seatbelts were new to me, with a five-point harness designed to hold occupants solidly in place when the aircraft flew upside down. Boggie demonstrated how to fasten them and then instructed me to cinch them down so tightly it bordered on uncomfortable. With a hint of what was to come, he added, "You'll be happy soon enough that these belts are snug."

The first thing that struck me was the fantastic visibility in the cockpit under the bubble canopy. The pilot's view was panoramic. I could see without restriction in front, above, and even behind me. Good visibility was key for safety and control. With the aircraft upside down or rolling—"unusual attitudes" they were called—pilots needed the ability to see in all directions to orient themselves to ground and horizon references.

After the required checks were completed, we took off for the training area. Once clear of the Bankstown control zone, Boggie got right down to business. After running through his pre-aerobatics checks on the airplane, he gave me the unflinching steely-eyed look of a fighter jock and asked evenly, "Are you ready?"

"You bet," I answered enthusiastically, although I had no idea what to expect.

"I'll show you a barrel roll first. It's nice and gentle, all positive Gs." Smoothly entering this introductory aerobatic maneuver, Boggie started to roll the aircraft while following a spiral course aligned with the direction of flight.

I could feel the G forces starting to build, pressing me into my seat. Looking at what would normally be up, I instead saw the ground as we went through inverted flight. Boggie continued the roll through a complete 360 degrees, until we were once again upright.

"That's amazing!" I nearly squealed with delight. "Let's do some more!"

Boggie obliged with some more rolls, followed by a loop-the-loop and then more complex maneuvers that had me literally dangling from my seatbelt, as the negative G-forces tugged on my body. Soon I was giggling, like a kid riding a rollercoaster for the first time. As we floated and tumbled through the air, I knew that I would never again be happy flying only straight and level.

Boggie told me to follow through on the controls before attempting some maneuvers myself. I took to it immediately and intuitively and found my first basic aerobatic tricks amazingly simple.

"Are you ready to do a spin?" he asked.

"Yeah, let's do it!"

Boggie talked me through the spin as if he were on automatic pilot. Seventy knots, sixty knots, approaching the stall, then back stick and full rudder . . . now! The aircraft responded immediately, first rolling upside-down and then settling into a constant rotation, as we hurtled earthward, the ground whirling around in a dizzying fashion.

Boggie called the airspeed and reminded me to look inside, not outside. He didn't want the spinning motion to make me sick. When it was time to recover, Boggie demonstrated the standard technique, taking his hands off the stick with a flourish and applying full rudder in the direction opposite the rotation. After a few turns, the aircraft stopped spinning abruptly, which left us pointing straight down toward the ground. There was an eerie silence. Because the spinning motion interrupted the fuel flow, the engine had stopped, and the propeller was no longer turning. The windshield was filled with the alarming view of a paddock below. As the ground grew nearer, I noticed a few cows milling among the trees.

Instinctively, I grabbed on to the instrument panel in front of me, my heart pounding. Without flinching, Boggie held SXY in a steep dive, relying on increasing airspeed to turn the propeller and restart the engine. I finally stopped holding my breath when the engine sputtered and roared back to life. It seemed not a moment too soon. What a rush!

I noticed that Boggie had to use a full boot of rudder to stop the spin and silently prayed that when it came to my turn to teach this, my leg would be strong enough to safely recover on my own. That would be something I'd have to deal with later.

The spin completed, we started to head back to the airport. But Boggie's pièce de résistance was soon to follow. I noticed a Tobago aircraft from my old school passing beside us. Over the radio, I heard that it was fellow instructor Herc with one of his students.

"Right, then. Let's have some fun!" Boggie said, when I told him who it was.

He called Herc on the radio and asked him to tune into a discreet radio frequency so that we could communicate in private. Once Herc complied, Boggie instructed him to maintain a steady heading and altitude.

What on earth is he planning?

Before I had time to think about it, Boggie pulled back on the stick, and the nose of our Robin pitched up and over as he began to execute a barrel roll over and around the Tobago! I couldn't stop laughing, as I glanced out of the canopy to see Herc's eyes widen. There was a look of utter disbelief on his face as he watched the little black Robin swirl around his aircraft. Though I couldn't be sure, it seemed to me I could see him mouth a few words of profanity before we completed our aerial show. This was certainly not something we covered in our instructor course, and I felt pretty certain we'd be admonished for it once we were back on the ground.

So, in my first aerobatics demo, Boggie threw everything at me that the little Robin could do. We darted around the clouds, dodging under and over them, perhaps a bit too close per regulation but fun nonetheless. My initiation over, we headed back to the flying school. I had loved every moment and was now solidly hooked. My introduction to aerobatics proved to be not at all unnerving and every bit as exciting as I'd imagined.

Back on the ground, I continued to ride the high of that first aerobatic flight with Boggie, and I could hardly wait for the chance to start working toward my endorsement. I was relieved that I didn't get nauseous when we'd "wrung out" that Robin, which is common for many pilots when they're first introduced to unusual attitudes—although I wondered if I should credit Boggie's skillful flying for my physical fortitude rather than the strength of my constitution. Either way, I took it as an auspicious start to my future as an aerobatics instructor.

After that day, I flew and studied every moment I could, and I succeeded in attaining my aerobatics rating. Although I was excited to show off my new skills to Mum and Dad, they politely refused. Flying upside-down wasn't for everyone! I relished my work as an aerobatics instructor, and my love for aviation deepened. It was as if a whole new aspect of flying had opened up to me. Even with all of my career progress and personal growth, one of the most interesting developments for me at SAS was yet to be revealed.

PART THREE

BLUE SKIES & TAILWINDS

I still feel fear, yet I am not afraid.

› 21 ‹

Teaching aerobatics at SAS was a crazy, fun-filled time, and I loved every minute. Flying had given me a new direction in life, a renewed sense of purpose that filled the void from my days as an aspiring athlete. It felt great to be part of a team again, and this sense of belonging was an important part of my healing. So, although I missed being able to run or to ski, I didn't dwell on my loss.

Being the only female instructor at the school, I was treated like one of the boys, which suited me just fine. It never occurred to me that there could be any romance because we were all friends. Besides, certain things about my body were still a bit of an unknown, and I wasn't ready to explore that part of my life just yet.

Despite my reluctance to consider dating, I found myself spending considerable time with one of the other instructors. Tim was always pulling practical jokes. He had a dry, laconic wit, the best of which passed right over the heads of the unobservant. He was also a gifted pilot with thousands of instructing hours under his belt. The turning point in our relationship occurred when Tim and I both had a few days off. He had access to an aircraft at a local airfield, and we decided to fly it to visit some friends of mine in the south. The Wilkensons lived in a small country town, not far from the snow-fields I knew well from my days as a ski racer.

When Tim pulled the Skybolt from the hangar, I could barely contain my excitement. Painted green and white, she was a taildragger with an open cockpit and tandem seating, and she was in pristine condition. I had never flown in a biplane before, but I eagerly climbed into the front cockpit. Tim helped me with the seatbelts—two for each occupant, a safety precaution for an aerobatic aircraft without a canopy. The headsets were sewn into an old-fashioned leather cap, like the Red Baron would have worn, which was charming and nostalgic. Assured that I was set, Tim strapped himself in, and we were ready for action.

With blue skies, light winds, and not a cloud in sight, it was a perfect day for flying. We wasted no time getting airborne and set a heading for Cooma. The open cockpit made it noisy and windy, which only added to my excitement and sense of adventure. Tim settled into an instructor's role and took me through some of Skybolt's idiosyncrasies. The rudder pedals were such a long way from my feet that I couldn't reach them. There was a joystick between my knees and only the most basic instruments in the panel, some new to me but nothing I couldn't handle. The Skybolt was built for aerobatics and not much else. We relied on the compass to tell us roughly what direction to head, but otherwise we went where our fancy took us.

We flew through the valleys at low level, zoomed over the mountains, and then dipped down once more on the other side of the ridges. Soon we spotted Cooma Airport in the distance, and Tim configured the Skybolt for our approach. Never having landed a taildragger, I noticed how the nose of the plane was higher than I was used to. Since we couldn't see a thing ahead of us, Tim kept her in a sideslip, one wing low, until we were just above the runway, at which point he kicked it straight with the rudder and set us down in a smooth landing.

June Wilkenson was a gentle and hardworking woman, typical of those who live on the land. She was waiting at the airport, ready to drive us back to her farm. Once there, we were served a hearty ranch lunch with the family, after which Tim went off with June's husband, Bob. I stayed behind with June. It had been a while since we'd visited, and we had a lot of catching up to do.

June's intuition was aroused, and she questioned me about Tim. But I shrugged it off as "just friends," with different interests at that.

"Sometimes that's the best way," she replied. "Opposites do attract," she added, with a hint that was hard to miss.

I wasn't ready to open up to June, to share my true reservations about entering any romantic, and ultimately physical, relationship, whether with Tim or anyone else. I was just beginning to feel comfortable on my own, learning to navigate the bewildering landscape of my injuries. I also didn't want to threaten the friendship Tim and I had cultivated. He seemed willing to leave it at that, too.

After dinner Tim and I studied our maps to plot the next day's route home. It would take us back over the mountains to the coastal town of Moruya. When our planning was done, we sat around the fire chatting with the Wilkenson family before retiring. Once I lay in bed, my thoughts drifted back to June's offhand comments and the possibility of a different relationship with Tim. But given all my bodily issues, how might that work?

The next day Tim and I said our goodbyes and headed back to the airport. Unlike the clear day we had when we began our trip, the weather for our return was overcast and threatening. As we approached the mountains, we were forced to fly around clouds scattered over the tops of the peaks in order to stay in the clear. Cold raindrops stung my face as we weaved among the clouds. I stretched out my arms into the chill and mist, savoring the experience. It was magical.

The beauty of Australia's varied and rugged landscapes struck me as we neared the coastal town of Moruya. One moment we were in the magnificent wild country of the Snowy Mountains, and then half an hour away by air, we were drinking in a bird's-eye view of the striking, expansive Pacific coastline. I inhaled the damp air of the propeller blast and rejoiced at my good fortune to be alive and treated to such a rich experience.

We'd planned an interim stop at an airstrip situated right on the shore. After we secured the plane, we walked over to the beach and sat on the sand. Soaking up the ocean view and the sounds of the surf was a stark contrast to the exhilaration of being airborne and dodging clouds only minutes earlier. Soon we launched for the final leg of our flight, following the coastline at low level. We startled a few sailboarders, not to mention the fishermen on the rock cliffs. They waved good-naturedly as we scooted past. I imagined their envy at the fun we were having.

Our trip together suggested to each of us that Tim and I had more in common than flying. We began to see more of each other, and our friendship deepened. Over time, I shared some of my fears with him, including those related to my body. I started to believe that maybe, despite my disability, I might just be ready to have a fulfilling physical and emotional relationship.

› 22 ‹

Tim had recently moved to a home that was closer to mine, which made it easy and natural to see each other more frequently. One day after we had finished flying, he asked if I would like to go out for dinner. I agreed and then headed home to change before he picked me up. We went to one of our favorite restaurants in Darling Harbour, in Sydney, which was located on the water's edge. We chatted about our day, which mostly revolved around flying, while I fiddled unconsciously with a heart-shaped ring I wore on my right hand.

"That's a nice ring," Tim commented.

I nodded. "A friend made it for me as a birthday present."

"I think we should do something about getting one for the other hand," he replied.

The remark sailed right over my head. "What was that?" I asked.

He looked me in the eye, "I said, 'What do you think about getting one for your left hand?'"

"Why?" I was oblivious to his hint.

He took both my hands into his and looked at me, a little nervously. His demeanor struck me as uncharacteristic. I wondered what might be on his mind.

"Janine, don't make this any harder for me than it is. I'm asking you to marry me."

"What did you say?"

"Will . . . you . . . marry . . . me?"

No misunderstanding that!

Although his proposal surprised me, I thought back to the conversations we'd had about my problems, my injuries, and the care I required. Despite all of that, he wanted to be with me—and I realized that I wanted to be with him.

Eight months later, we married in a simple ceremony surrounded by friends and family. Even though the medical experts cast doubt over the extent of my injuries and whether they would allow me to have children, I was pregnant not long after our wedding. Tim and I were thrilled, as were our families and friends.

From the beginning, it was apparent my pregnancy would be no run-of-the-mill affair. First, there was the added risk of urinary tract infections, to which I remained especially vulnerable. Then, there were the purely mechanical aspects of carrying a child: I might have to wear a brace throughout the pregnancy to ensure that my spine could withstand the extra pressure.

And no one could predict how my body would stand up to labor if I attempted a conventional delivery. For starters, I didn't have normal pelvic tone, the muscular strength to push the baby out in the final stages. There was my fused vertebral column, which eliminated flexion in my lower spine and added to the challenge for both my baby and me. Little about my pregnancy and delivery could be predicted to follow the book, and there was the very real possibility of a caesarean delivery.

The stresses on my body from flying aerobatics were also not recommended for an expectant mother. The demands of pregnancy combined with those associated with my injuries meant that I tired easily, too. It soon became apparent that continuing to work at SAS would not be practical, so I hung up my headsets after my first trimester to focus entirely on my pregnancy.

By the time I reached full term, my weight was up by only twenty-two pounds, the lowest acceptable weight gain for a woman my size. My back was starting to act up, which came as no surprise to anyone. I had difficulty getting around as my compromised legs struggled to cope with the extra burden. Many of the dire predictions of my medical team seemed to be coming true.

I was scheduled to have my baby at King George V Memorial Hospital's new birthing center in Camperdown, a short drive from our home. My obstetrician, Sue, was a bit hesitant at first about this choice. Camperdown was a modern center designed for low-risk pregnancies, and she doubted whether they would accept me. But I persevered. I longed to start motherhood with a normal delivery of my child.

Labor started on Valentine's Day 1991. I checked into the birthing center on a humid summer's night. Once registered and settled into the comparative comfort of my room, I tried everything possible, with the midwife's help, to alleviate the pain. Along with the contractions, nausea caused me to vomit at regular intervals, so I split my time between the bathroom and the bedroom during this vigil. Seeing my discomfort, the midwife recommended a move to the spa, where she hoped warm water could take some of the pressure off my body and provide relief. She put on some classical music and dimmed the lights, but nothing helped to dim the pain.

My contractions became almost unbearable, each lasting two-and-a-half minutes with only a twenty-second respite before the next one came on. What concerned all of us most was that the baby had begun to move down the birth canal to create tremendous pressure on the area where I had the vertebral fusion. The pain became so intense that I feared my compromised spine wouldn't be able to endure the stress. With no way to relieve the mounting pressure, the pain grew intolerable. Due to my complicated history, an injection of numbing medication into the spinal area (an epidural) would be too risky, and my persistent nausea ruled out nitrous oxide gas. I was left with no choice but to bear it.

The short breaks between contractions gave me no time to relax. I steeled myself, hoping the next contraction wouldn't strike with as much ferocity. "I can't take another one," I would gasp. I tried reminding myself that I had endured pain much worse than this.

"Just one more," Tim would say, consoling me.

This exchange became our delivery litany. In this way, with Tim's support, I managed to bear labor beyond the transition stage, and we moved back into the bedroom. Tim pulled up the window shades, which revealed blinding bright sunshine. "It's a lovely day," he observed. My eyes tried to adjust to the sunlight. I hadn't realized I had been in labor all night.

By morning, the staff had changed shifts. Now a midwife named Geraldine was stationed at my side. The natural pushing urge never came on—likely because of my spinal cord damage—leaving me to conjure whatever resources I could to encourage the baby to deliver. I was sitting on a birthing stool when the obstetrician came to check on my progress.

"Please, get the baby out," I pleaded. "My back can't take any more."

"Janine, I can get the forceps if you want, but . . ."

I didn't want to hear her explanation. This had to end, and soon. "Get them, please. Just get it out!" I screamed.

Hearing my urgency, the obstetrician ran to fetch the forceps. Geraldine looked at me compassionately but spoke firmly: "Janine, if she gets the forceps you'll have to get up and walk to the bed. You'll have to lie on your back, and the pain will be even worse."

Even worse?

My back already felt as if it were breaking. I looked over at the bed, overwhelmed by the thought of struggling to stand and walk even that short distance. Now, at the brink of what stress my back could bear, I mustered all my strength. *Please baby, come out.* I bore down with newfound intensity and gritted my teeth. I had to push this baby out.

"Janine, that's great. Almost there. One more," I heard Geraldine urge.

Once again, I summoned the determination I'd practiced as an athlete. *Come on. You're almost there.* I closed my eyes and gave one last all-out effort. In that final, momentous heave, I felt a tremendous relief as the pain instantly drained from my body.

"That's it! You've done it!" Geraldine exclaimed. "It's a girl, Janine. You have a beautiful baby girl!"

I looked down to see Geraldine cradling a child—my child. It was over. I—we—had crossed yet another finish line with a win. I held out my arms, and Geraldine passed the newborn to me. She was slimy, bawling, and more beautiful than I could have imagined. Through the blur of my tears, I could see she was extraordinary. In that moment, I was overwhelmed with a depth of love I'd never imagined. Annabel was my miracle, and together we beat the odds.

› 23 ‹

In the year following Annabel's birth, we moved to the country town of Tamworth, a five-hour drive north of Sydney. Tim secured a job with a regional airline, the next step for a pilot seeking a position with a major carrier like Qantas. This was the first time since my accident that I lived such a long distance from my family, as well as my medical team. In so many ways, I was starting a new chapter of my life.

Though I kept my certificates current, there was not nearly enough free time for me to continue giving flight instruction. When Tim was away flying, I was home with Annabel. I marveled at how a baby could occupy so much time. Feeding, bathing, playing, and sleeping, Annabel kept me busy. I was exhausted, but I was content and wanted for nothing.

If being married gave me a sense of security, then becoming a mother fulfilled me. During those first months, I desired nothing more than to cradle Annabel in my arms as we gazed into each other's eyes. I was besotted with this baby. Before my time with her, I could not have imagined experiencing so profound a love.

By this time, five years had passed since my accident, and I decided that this was the perfect chance to write about my experience. My desire to do so developed out of a need for catharsis, but no less important, it would provide a medium to share my experiences with others who had experienced deep loss. I remembered how during my recovery I longed to learn about spinal cord injury from those who had been through similar ordeals, but at the time, there were few books in which I could find information or solace. I hoped that writing my story might help others gain the sense of normalcy I'd had to cultivate through trial and error for both my physical and emotional rehabilitation.

I wrote and mailed a twenty-page synopsis to various publishing houses to gauge interest. After receiving several polite rejections, I decided that the best option was to pick up the phone and call one of the major publishing houses in Australia: Pan Macmillan. No one told me that this wasn't the way it was normally done, so I was oblivious to the fact that I might have made things easier and more professional had I employed a literary agent.

The conversation went something like this: "I have a compelling story, and I'd like to offer it to your company first." Surprisingly, I was put through to the acquisitions editor, Jane Palfreyman, who agreed to meet with me the following day.

During our meeting, Jane sat transfixed as I told her about my experience. She assured me that she would read my synopsis and call me the following week. As it turned out, she phoned the very next day to tell me that she and her boss would like to discuss my story with me at a coffee shop near my home. And just like that, I had my first book deal, and writing *Never Tell Me Never* began in earnest.

Putting my story down on paper proved more of a challenge than I'd considered because it forced me to relive so many painful events. I also had to sift through and organize mounds of material spanning my girlhood to motherhood: photos, letters, medical records, and various memorabilia. At times I found myself overwhelmed with emotions such as loss and grief. There were days when I was unable to motivate myself to write so much as a word. Even when I was less triggered by the sadness, I couldn't bear to proofread what I'd written. Instead, I printed each page as I typed it and placed it unedited and face down in the growing pile that was taking shape as my manuscript.

With the persistence befitting an endurance athlete, I navigated this new emotional minefield, as well as managed the demands of caring for Annabel, and submitted my first draft just before Christmas 1993. Well into my second pregnancy and distracted with the demands common to a young family, I didn't give much thought to how my book might alter the course of my life.

The following March, after another difficult and protracted labor, I gave birth to another beautiful baby girl, Charlotte Rose. She was fair, like Annabel, but she had a wisp of red hair. Unlike Annabel though, she didn't cry when I first held her, but instead looked straight into my eyes with a wise and knowing look, as if to say, "Hey, what took you so long?"

› 24 ‹

Just before *Never Tell Me Never* was due to be released, my story was picked up in Australia by the popular show *60 Minutes*. It turned out that my old friend Ado had since evolved his practice to become a celebrity doctor on the TV show *Survivor*, and he rang his producer friend Stephen Taylor to tell him my story. In turn, Stephen assigned the famous and popular reporter Charles Wooley to be the presenter. Filming was scheduled to start immediately.

For the next two weeks, I spent every waking moment with the *60 Minutes* film crew and field production team. Being forced to relive parts of my former life presented me with an unexpected gift: I now realized just how content I felt with my life in present time. I relished being a wife and a mother as much as I had the chance to compete at the Olympics. Indeed, when Charles asked me directly about missing my chance to stand on the podium for Australia, I answered without a second thought, "I won my gold medal. I have my family." The editors of the program chose this exchange to be the poignant ending of the segment.

I enjoyed filming with the team, and it seemed Charles did, too—at least he did until we went to the airport. He was unapologetic about his dislike for small aircraft, and he was demonstrably dismayed at the prospect of flying upside-down in one with a partial paraplegic at the controls. When Charles arrived at the airport on the day we were scheduled to fly together, I could see he was pale and nervous.

"I hope you know what you're doing, Shepherd. I'm not looking forward to this!"

"Oh, don't worry Charles. It'll be great fun. I haven't done much flying in ages, and I'm really looking forward to getting back at the controls." I laughed inwardly, having some fun at his expense, letting him think my piloting skills might have gotten a bit rusty.

The film crew rigged a camera on top of the instrument panel, to capture the expressions on our faces while in flight. Both Charles and

I were set up with mics to record the audio. A chase plane would film the Robin as I put her through a gentle aerobatic routine. My unwilling passenger grew ever more unsure about what he'd gotten himself into.

I had to be mindful not to let the film crew distract me from the protocol of a meticulous and safe pilot. After I'd gone through my pre-flight inspections as required, we climbed in the cockpit. As I secured and cinched tight his seatbelt, Charles asked an obvious question.

"So, if you have no feeling in your legs, how do you control your feet on the pedals?" His apprehension was now clearly apparent.

I looked at him with a wry smile and paused just a bit for dramatic effect. "Actually, I just put my feet on the pedals and hope for the best," I laughed. But he didn't.

With cameras rolling, we taxied to the runway to get our clearance and depart for the training area. Once we were airborne and at a safe altitude, I went through the requisite pre-aerobatic checks and pronounced us ready. Dismissing the anxious expression on Charles's face as his hamming it up for the camera, I cleared the area for our first maneuver.

"Okay. Ready? Here we go!" I announced with a flourish, as I smoothly pulled back on the joystick to start a loop. My gaze was fixed outside the aircraft. The horizon was soon replaced with only blue sky as the Robin's nose reached for vertical. With a touch of right rudder over the top, the picture outside reversed, and ground view now filled the windscreen. I held a constant stick position until I felt the familiar bump that comes from completing the circle and passing through my own wake, which meant we were again flying level.

With a scant pause to transition to the next maneuver, I again pulled the aircraft up to a perfectly vertical climb for the hammerhead turn. I watched as the airspeed dropped to forty knots, my cue to boot in enough left rudder to turn the nose 180 degrees. With a brisk pivot, we retraced the direction we'd climbed—only now we were heading straight down.

Now gaining speed on a perfect vertical down line, I adjusted the stick pressure to maintain our track. Reaching eighty knots, I reduced power and pulled out of the dive, again momentarily returning to level flight.

"Woo-hoo!" I yelled with sheer delight, above the roar of the engine. "How much fun was that!"

My passenger did not in the least return my enthusiasm. "I feel sick! That's enough. Can we please go home?" Charles fairly begged.

"Oh, come on Charles," I cajoled, "we haven't yet gotten enough footage for the cameras. The producer said we had to film an entire aerobatic routine."

He reluctantly agreed, but after a few more maneuvers, he strongly insisted that we land. "Please," he pleaded. "I'll do anything. I'll promote your bloody book, *just get me down!*" As if to underscore his point that there would be no further negotiation on his demand, he reached behind the seat and pressed the off button on the camera—a moment the editors found amusing enough to include in the final broadcast.

I realized he wasn't joking and opened the air vent to help forestall his nausea. Then I immediately turned back to the aerodrome.

Charles leaned back, double-checking the camera, and then gave me a crestfallen look. "Oh no, I don't believe it!" he exclaimed. "The damned camera didn't work. We got none of that on film!" A look of utter disbelief clouded his face. "I don't care what Taylor says. I'm not going back up to do that again!"

Once we landed and taxied back to the flying school, Charles sheepishly explained what happened to Stephen, the producer.

"Oh well, if it hasn't come out, you'll have to go up and do it again," Stephen casually replied, either oblivious to Charles's fear or having a bit of fun with it.

Fortunately for Charles, the video had been recorded, and he was spared the dreaded do-over. In fact, we captured some extraordinary footage of the flight, including shots of Charles's face contorted into a look of pure terror. What was disappointing, though, was that his screams of profanity, which had punctuated the routine, were inaudible.

In what proved to be exceptionally fortunate timing, the *60 Minutes* segment, titled "Survival of the Fittest," aired right as my book hit the shelves. From that moment, my life took a more frenzied turn.

By Christmas, the first printing of my book had sold out, and several management agencies expressed interest in representing my career—not as an author but as an inspirational speaker. I signed on with several booking agencies, and before long I found myself traveling the country—indeed, the globe—addressing myriad corporate organizations on the speaking circuit. A fledgling in this career, I crossed paths with many seasoned speakers who became my mentors and offered generous support and advice. I was grateful for the camaraderie, and I learned a great deal from each of them.

Adding to this flurry of interest, I fielded inquiries into securing rights for a film adaptation of my book, an exciting prospect but way beyond my expertise. Quite by chance, I was put in contact with a movie producer named David Elfick, who lived in a neighboring village. David dropped by our house to pick up a copy of my book. I had been out of the hospital only a few weeks after yet another operation on one of my feet, so I greeted him on crutches, with one leg in a cast. "Oh, don't worry," I assured him. "It was just time for a tune-up and an oil change!"

I grew to like and trust David immensely as we worked together over the next few months, exploring the best options for the film. The first step in making a feature-length movie was to find the ideal writer for the screenplay. Nearly a year had passed before I got an excited call from David telling me he'd found the right person, a scriptwriter from South Africa named John Cundill.

John warned me that I would have my work cut out for me. "Janine, this isn't the sort of story where I retreat to the mountains and return with a finished manuscript. We are going to be spending a lot of time together." True to his admonition, John—with his computer in tow—became a regular visitor to our busy and noisy household.

Educating John on my life journey began in earnest with a visit to Prince Henry Hospital, a field trip that proved to be an eye-opener for me as well as for him. He found the setting desolate and despairing, emotions that were amplified by an aged facility facing the possibility of closure. Many of the buildings had already been abandoned. For me, walking into acute spinal again, after eleven years, was like stepping back in time, although much had changed since my stint there. It had once been an active ward, bustling with medical staff. Now, many of the beds were empty. I pointed out my old bed to John and even managed to catch up with the few familiar staff who still worked there.

Despite the dilapidated appearance of the ward and my flood of emotions, coming back to the acute spinal on my own two feet had its positive side. I was proud at how far I had come since being strapped to that now-empty bed. I had learned to fly, gotten married, and become a mother. I was walking about the very ward where doctors had debated whether I'd be spending the rest of my life in a wheelchair. My book was well on its way to national best-seller status, and I was in the company of a screenwriter working to bring my story to film. Best of all, I was pregnant with our third child!

While John finished up with details of the screenplay, David was busy casting the characters. In the midst of all this, I went into the hospital and gave birth to a baby boy, Angus. His fair features and coloring, much like Charlotte's, reflected his father's Irish lineage. My dad was thrilled to finally get the boy he had always wanted, a grandson for him to spoil. Angus was going to bring an interesting dimension to our family, and with his birth, our family now felt complete.

Some weeks later, filming on *Never Tell Me Never* was scheduled to begin. I met with the Australian actor Claudia Karvan, who had been selected to play me. It's an extraordinary experience to talk with someone who has been cast to play your character in a movie. It was a treat for her, too, because Claudia had yet to play someone who was still living. We struck up an instant rapport.

David wanted to get the main characters and their actor counterparts together so that each cast member could get a feel for the real-life person they would be playing. I organized a barbecue at my house a few weeks before principal photography began and invited friends and family to meet their actor counterparts. By the start of production, the snow was starting to melt, which gave shooting the ski scenes top priority. One of the challenges we faced was finding a skier who would be both technically competent and convincing as a stand-in double for Claudia. We also needed a second skier to ski against "me" in the race scenes. Fortunately, many of my skiing friends were happy for a chance to have their moments of film fame.

While I was occupied with my family duties, the field crew reported a brilliant week in the snow: ideal weather and near perfect conditions for shooting. Claudia had never skied, but the consummate professional she was, she fervently took to her lessons with my friend and instructor, Pab. Curious to hear how things had gone on the set, I rang Claudia the first night at the ski lodge.

"How were your first lessons, Claudia?"

"I hate cross-country skiing," she replied flatly.

I was shattered. How could she play the part of an Olympic hopeful ski racer if she didn't in the least like the sport? A wave of concern washed over me. I felt sympathy for this acclaimed actress getting a role that early in production was already proving challenging for her.

But then Pab got on the phone and reassured me that despite her protestations, Claudia had done well and was proving to be a natural. Almost as an afterthought, Pab mentioned that working with Claudia reminded him of the days skiing with the real-life Janine.

"When I told Claudia it was time to pack it in for the day, she refused to leave the snow. She wouldn't quit. She's as bloody determined as you, Machine!" Pab beamed.

As it would turn out, no sooner was she into the second day of training than Claudia did an about-face and became consumed with her enjoyment of cross-country skiing.

David rang me each night with an update on the day's shoot. He knew how much I wished I could be present for the filming. He assured me that my racing spirit was alive on the snow and that they were all thinking of me.

After the skiing scenes were shot, the set moved to Macquarie University Gymnasium, near enough to home for me to attend the first day of shooting. I arrived to find organized chaos. Actors, extras, crew, cameras, even production trucks were moving about with dizzying urgency. The action on set starkly contrasted with the real-life Janine Shepherd, who was pushing Angus in his stroller, with her other two small children in tow. The real-life subject of this film now looked very much out of place in an athletic scene. David introduced me to many of the crew and gave me a tour of the set. Settling into a chair behind the cameras, I found myself in the most remarkable and bewildering position of watching complete strangers act out my life story.

The very next day, close to my house, they were shooting the accident scene. With Annabel and Charlotte at school, I packed up little Angus and headed off to have a look at the set. As I made my way up to the re-created scene of the accident, I caught my first glimpse of Claudia. She'd been outfitted in bike gear identical to what I'd been wearing on the day of the accident. Sprawled on the ground, her body and head were covered in simulated blood and gravel, and her clothes were torn. Suddenly I was overwhelmed, transported back to that horrible day in 1986. My mind flooded with awful memories as I realized that watching this scene being filmed wasn't such a great idea after all. I hurried to my car with Angus and drove straight home.

The filming of the hospital scenes was equally difficult for me to observe. I had no recollection of the day I had arrived at Prince Henry, but seeing Claudia on a stretcher, outfitted exactly as I'd been, was nothing short of breathtaking. Just as I watched her limp body being loaded into an ambulance, she turned her head, looked right at me, and stuck out her tongue. I couldn't help but laugh, grateful for the levity—and for the compassion and respect Claudia continued to offer me throughout the filming.

Of particular importance to both David and me was casting real-life patients for the hospital scenes. This made the film more authentic and created a deeper, more meaningful connection for the cast and crew. We engaged twenty former spinal patients. Some of them, including Maria, had also been in ward one during the toughest times of my recovery.

After weeks of shooting and months of planning, filming was at last complete. David threw a huge wrap party to celebrate, inviting all the real-life extras from the hospital to join cast and crew. We partied and danced for hours, some in wheelchairs. The next morning I glanced at my feet to find them bruised and nearly flattened, run over by wheelchair-operators caught up in the frenzied festivities.

The finished film debuted in 1998 and was broadcast on national TV. Family and friends gathered in my home to watch the premiere. Excited, David rang me the following morning to tell me that it had topped prime-time ratings. Everyone who saw it agreed that *Never Tell Me Never* accurately and convincingly captured the story of my life—a roller-coaster ride that would soon take yet another dramatic twist.

› 25 ‹

Tim and I had always dreamed of living on a farm. Hopeful that the time might soon come, I figured it would be a good idea for my grade-school girls to get a jumpstart on life outside of the city and learn to ride horses. Annabel started her lessons at age seven, with Charlotte following in short order. They began their drills under the watchful eye of a wonderful and accomplished teacher, Sandy, whose mounts for the lessons were two small ponies, Owie and Squizzie.

Never having been around horses or equestrian communities, I had to come up to speed with the various gear and jargon. I enjoyed watching the girls' lessons and soaked up Sandy's instructions with great enthusiasm: "toes to heaven," "heels to hell," "birds' heads up," "stretch up tall," "shorten your reins." These phrases, unique to the riding world, soon became as indelibly marked in my memory as the many aviation terms I learned as both a student and an instructor.

Once Sandy was satisfied that both girls could consistently demonstrate proficient and safe horsemanship, the next step was to teach them how to jump. Watching these advanced lessons was a real test of my motherly instincts, but with Sandy's expert tutelage, both Annabel and Charlotte were soon expertly sailing over jumps of all shapes and sizes.

Seeing how well they took to the sport, we bought our own horse, a fluffy, white 12.2-hand pony named Toby, whom we all adopted as the newest member of our family. "Pony Club" outings became a regular weekend event for us. Saturday before each meet, we'd clean everything: tack, bridles, saddles, clothes, and boots. Sunday morning, we would load Toby in the trailer and head to the grounds for a day of competition.

Intrigued by the girls' progress, I eventually decided it was time to put my fear aside and take some lessons myself. I began my training on Owie, a pony so small that my feet were practically dragging along the ground when I was mounted. Despite his diminutive stature, I was initially guarded and tentative, dreading the thought of a fall.

My anxiety was only part of the challenge. With no feeling in my backside, I couldn't tell how I was situated in the saddle. I had to consciously dismiss the distinct sense that I was about to topple off at any moment. The lack of feeling and strength in my feet also meant I struggled to keep them squarely in the stirrups. Sandy came up with the brilliant idea of tying my feet in the stirrups with elastic bands, so that if I did fall, the bands would merely snap and my feet would easily release.

After mastering the basics, I graduated from the ponies to the bigger horses in Sandy's stable. Even though I was still just riding in the arena, I was free of the training aid called the lunge rope and could ride completely on my own. I had also progressed from a trot to a canter, a pace that was much more comfortable and rhythmic.

One day while I was riding around the arena, Sandy casually mentioned a young student trainee who also had a disability. "Janine, did you know they have competitive horseback riding in the Paralympics?" she asked offhandedly, as I trotted around the arena. "I think you should get classified and compete."

I had never before considered the Paralympics. After my accident, I wanted to distance myself completely from any athletic competition. At any rate, flying had compensated for the tremendous disappointment of missing my bid for the Olympics. Sandy's prompting, though, set me to wondering. Maybe enough time had passed, or maybe the competitor in me had simply reemerged. It didn't take long for me to mull it over. Before the lesson was up, I had agreed with Sandy to give dressage competition a go!

In order to be competitive, I'd have to have a suitable horse. Before long I found her, the perfect companion and training partner. Jacananda Tisharni, or Sharni, was a quarter horse, standing fourteen hands tall. She wasn't exactly the ideal dressage mount, but her gentle temperament and manageable size suited me well at this budding stage of my riding career.

The next step was to get classified, meaning I'd be eligible for Riding for the Disabled (RDA) competitions. RDA encompasses four grades, each reflecting a level of increased ability. Although by then I was comfortable riding at a level somewhere between grades three and four, I got classified as the higher of the two, which meant I had my work cut out for me. Aside from that, how was my little Sharni going to perform at this elite level? It was going to be a stretch for horse and rider alike to take on seasoned grade-four competitors at this point in our respective careers.

Over the next few months, Sandy, Sharni, and I prepared tirelessly for our first competition, a simple preliminary test in a dressage event scheduled for able-bodied riders.

I spent the night before the event cleaning my gear and packing everything I anticipated needing for our big day. Harking back to my meticulous preparation for flying practices, I diligently went over the last-minute details of Sharni's debut, grooming her whiskers, painting her hoofs black, and brushing her coat. Early the next morning, I drove to the stables, loaded Sharni into the trailer, and headed off to pick up Sandy on the way to the showground.

Once we offloaded Sharni and saddled her up, our first move was to the warm-up arena to get ready for the test. Most of the other horses there were at least seventeen hands tall—thoroughbreds and warmbloods. Next to these statuesque competitors, Sharni looked more like a pony. Just before our designated time to enter the arena, I made one last check of the elastic bands holding my feet in the stirrups and then waited my turn.

I was given the call to enter the arena and begin my routine. When all was said and done, I made a few mistakes but managed to remember the entire test, so both Sandy and I agreed it was a fine first showing. I scored respectably, and our modest success at this first event made me hungrier to improve my skills—and my scores—for the next event. I was surprised by how quickly I reconnected with the competitive spirit that I had placed on hold for so long.

For the remainder of that year, Sharni and I tackled able-bodied competitions, as well as those for riders with disabilities. In many ways, riding mirrored my love for flying. Dressage required a certain finesse that served to advance my riding skills immensely, just as aerobatics had elevated my performance as a pilot.

› 26 ‹

In late 2000, Tim and I purchased our dream home, an old weather-board cottage situated on a hundred acres of rolling pastures, in the picturesque Southern Highlands, not far from where he had grown up. Tim had been flying for Qantas for five years, allowing him greater flexibility in bidding for his trips. His ample time off meant that one of us could always be at home with the kids, which gave me the ability to travel to my speaking engagements. A few months before our move, Tim received the offer to upgrade from second to first officer with the airline; his training would begin immediately.

The course for first officer indoctrination was slated to take two months, leaving plenty of time for completion before our scheduled move to the new farm. For reasons unclear to me, though, training dragged on well past the anticipated completion. Tim had yet to finish as the day of our move approached. His last test—flying one leg from Sydney to Brisbane for an overnight stay, and then on to Singapore before heading home—was finally underway when he called me from Brisbane the night of his layover.

"Hey, honey. How'd it go?" I asked.

"Not great," he answered, his tone somber.

"What do you mean?"

"I don't know what's wrong, but I'm having some problems . . ." His voice trailed off.

"What sort of problems?"

"I don't know. Things just aren't working."

"But you passed the leg, didn't you?"

"Well, this leg doesn't count. The captain isn't sure what's wrong either."

It was heartbreaking to hear the despair in his voice, so I tried to console him, reminding him how close he was to completing his qualifications.

"Yeah, it will be okay. I'll call tomorrow night," he promised.

When the phone finally did ring the next night, I was unprepared for the news I received.

"I didn't finish. Captain is sending me home. I had to take sick leave," Tim said, his dejection nearly palpable through the phone line.

"What do you mean, 'sick'? What's wrong?"

"I'm not sure, but I'm not able to finish the flight. I'll be commuting home in the morning." That cryptic summary was all he offered in explanation.

"Tim, are you really okay?"

"I don't know what's happening. It wasn't working, so I'll be home tomorrow. I'll have to see the company doctor," he added.

My heart sank as I listened to his vague "explanation." I was confused about the exact nature of his ailment and worried for him. Tim had always excelled in his training. What in the world could have changed now, on the very last task?

That night I tossed and turned, wracking my brain as to what might have gone wrong in his flight check. Whatever it was, it must be serious for Tim to take sick leave so close to completing his FO qualification and upgrade.

When he arrived home, he looked worn out—his face sallow and his eyes bloodshot. I put my arms around him and gave him a hug.

"It's okay. You just need some rest," I offered reassuringly.

Weeks passed with Tim on extended leave from the airline, spending most of the time in bed. Even after the long-awaited examinations by the company doctor, we remained in the dark. His illness was mysterious and maddeningly hard to diagnose. It seemed not even the medical experts could offer any insight into what could be wrong or what might have happened during the check flight.

I remained as busy as ever, getting the kids organized, preparing and giving speeches, trying to get on top of the unpacking from our move, all the while trying to care for my husband's baffling affliction as best I could.

Tim was, indeed, tired, both physically and mentally, but there was something more dire that I couldn't quite put my finger on.

He was withdrawn and preferred to be alone. When I tried to question him about what had happened on his test flight, he wasn't forthcoming. Unable to offer any constructive help to nudge Tim out of his doldrums, I patiently waited it out, even though I wasn't at all sure what I was waiting for. At some indefinite, gnawing level, I grew concerned that something profound was happening to our lives.

I contacted Ado and openly discussed Tim's behavior and symptoms with him. As both friend and physician, Ado expressed concern that perhaps we were seeking the wrong kind of help.

"Nene, if you don't take Tim to someone who is qualified in the area of mental health, I am going to come down and drag him there myself," Ado told me. "I have a friend, Max, who might be able to get to the bottom of this. He's a psychiatrist, an expert physician who deals with these sorts of problems."

"A psychiatrist? Isn't this a simple case of exhaustion?"

"Perhaps, Nene, but I think it's worth getting Max's opinion."

I trusted Ado and his counsel, although I wasn't yet convinced we needed that sort of specialist. At Ado's urging, I agreed to see how Tim felt about the idea. They'd been friends for years. Tim trusted Ado, and there was a mutual respect between the two. So Tim agreed to see Max, and I rang the doctor's office and made an appointment. He decided to drive up to Max's office in Sydney on his own. I stayed with the kids.

It was afternoon when Tim arrived back home. I was anxious to hear how the visit had gone. I found him in the kitchen, staring out the window.

"How was your visit with Max?" I ventured.

Tim continued his gaze out the window, unresponsive.

"Tim, how was the appointment?"

He mumbled something I couldn't make out and still wouldn't look at me.

"I didn't hear you."

I looked across to where Tim was standing and saw that he'd returned with medication, numerous packets of pills. I picked up one of the packets and started to read the description.

"What is this all about?" I asked, "Surely you don't need all this medication."

He wheeled around to face me and smashed his mug into the sink. "How would you know?" He stormed out the door, slamming it behind him.

I was stunned and speechless at his response. His anger and uncharacteristic outburst frightened me, as did the packets of pills on the counter.

I walked on eggshells for the remainder of the day. I didn't dare bring up the subject of the doctor's visit until after the kids were in bed. Calmer now, Tim explained that the doctor was confident in prescribing the medication and that I should call his office for a complete description of what was happening.

Tim was asleep when I climbed into bed that night. I turned over and buried my face in my pillow. *Please, God, don't let this be happening to us,* I prayed as tears soaked my pillow. *Don't take Tim from me, from our family.*

When I reached Max the next day, he described Tim's breakdown in detail and told me why he felt Tim needed the medication. I didn't waste any time challenging his assessment. The diagnosis didn't seem fitting.

"Yes, I understand your reluctance to accept this," Max patiently replied, "but it isn't as simple as that. Just as there are many shades of gray, so, too, there are many degrees to mental illness. If it's any consolation, Tim's is a straightforward case. There's nothing complicated about it. It is treatable with medication."

Straightforward or not, I stayed my course in pressing this doctor to defend his diagnosis. It simply made no sense to me.

"But after just one consultation, how could you be certain?" I pressed.

"Janine, I've had a lot of experience in this area." Max was undeterred.

"But there were no warning signs," I pointed out. "All of a sudden, Tim got sick while at work, in the cockpit. That's all."

"I understand you may be struggling with my findings. Hearing this isn't easy. It never is. But I also have to tell you up front that Tim's illness is going to be pretty tough on you and your family." He added, "To be candid, not many marriages survive something like Tim is facing."

With those ominous words ringing in my ears, a mixture of defensiveness and resolve welled up from inside me.

"That isn't us," I told him defiantly. "I love Tim, and I can assure you our marriage will survive. We will beat this."

› 27 ‹

Other than caring for my children, my riding was the thing that kept me grounded during the difficulties of Tim's sick leave. In the saddle, I was able to retreat into my own world, transcending the reality of what our family was going through. Given the inherent danger, I was forced to concentrate solely on my riding whenever on my mount, and that proved cathartic for me.

I also knew I needed to keep the momentum going with my training if I was to achieve my goal of making the Paralympic team. Since we'd moved, I made some inquiries around the area and settled on a highly qualified riding coach named Jenny Delamont. She was regarded as one of the best in equestrian circles. During our first meeting, we sat around my kitchen table and discussed my ambition to be selected for the next Paralympics. Jenny drew up a plan, based on my riding skills to date, and charted the most efficient progression from there to reach the expertise required to achieve my goal.

In our first sessions, Jenny quickly uncovered deficiencies in my general horsemanship skills. If I was to ride at a level high enough to qualify for Paralympics, I first needed to know how to properly train my horse. I appreciated from the beginning of our work together that Jenny's coaching was turning me into a horsewoman, as well as elevating my talents as a dressage rider.

Not long after our lessons began, I entered an open competition in the nearby town of Goulburn. I was riding in a preliminary test—one of the entry-level tests for dressage—but I was pretty pleased just to be competing on the able-bodied circuit. After arriving at the showground and off-loading Sharni, I went over to the far side of the ground and lunged her, just as Jenny had taught me. I then got into the saddle and went through my warm-up, preparing for the test. As the time to perform my routine approached, I completed the last few preparations and made my way up to the arena.

The test went smoothly, although Sharni was up to her old trick of not keeping her head rounded, a clear sign to the judges that she was resisting the bit and being disobedient. So I was stunned when the results came out: I took first place! Coming home that day, excited and pleased with our performance, I proudly hung my blue ribbon up on the wall of the tack room as a talisman for keeping in mind my ultimate goal.

Soon it was time to move on to a horse capable of taking me to the next level, so I put out a call to the disabled rider circles. Before long, I found Rock of Gibraltar, or Rocky, a beautiful thoroughbred already trained in dressage.

Rocky arrived by horse transport late at night, well after the kids were asleep. Tim was in Sydney, so I had to off-load Rocky on my own. When the driver let down the ramp on the trailer, I could see Rocky's large shape looming in the darkness. He stood a stunning 16.3 hands high, and I was terrified at the prospect of handling such a big horse.

"Okay, ready to take him?" the driver asked.

"I think so," I answered, hesitantly.

The massive horse walked calmly down the ramp and stood before me, his gentle demeanor belying his stature.

"My God, he's huge!" I gasped.

The driver handed the lead rope to me, and I stood transfixed, in awe of this imposing steed. In the darkness he appeared even bigger than I had imagined. The poor animal had been standing in a truck for hours and had no idea where he was. As Rocky was clearly unsettled, I turned him loose in the paddock and went back to the house, wondering how I was ever going to muster up the courage to ride him.

Early the next morning, I went up to see how Rocky was adapting to his new surroundings. The first glimpse of him took my breath away. He was trotting around the arena, throwing his head about, and snorting loudly, as if to announce his arrival to my world. With each enormous stride, he looked to be floating on air, and I had never before seen a horse move with such grace. Transfixed, I watched him prancing about as if showing off his magnificence. I fell in love with him that instant.

Jenny couldn't wait to see him, and when she did, she, too, was suitably impressed. She rode him around the paddock for some time before declaring it my turn. Rocky's towering height, coupled with the fact that I was unable to stand on my toes, required me to climb onto a crate to maneuver into the saddle. Even then it was a challenge.

"Just walk him around for a while until you get comfortable," Jenny advised, adding a cautionary note to ensure that "his brakes" were working, too.

Rocky had a commanding walk, but it was surprisingly comfortable. *Okay, that's not too bad. Let's see what happens when I push him into a trot.*

When Jenny perceived my intent, she shouted a warning, "Careful, Janine. His trot is pretty big!"

I pushed aside my fear and urged Rocky on. He nearly bounced me out of the seat! "Yeah, you're right!" I hollered back to Jenny, clinging desperately to the saddle, trying to stay put. I hung in until I could manage to rise to his trot around the paddock without too much trouble. In stature and movement alike, everything about Rocky was outsized, but I soon relaxed with confidence in his gentlemanly nature and even temperament.

"That's good, Janine. Ready to try a canter?" Jenny suggested.

I applied the standard pressure with my legs that Rocky had been taught to perceive as the command to advance his pace. I was relieved to find that at canter, Rocky had a beautiful gait, one that I could sit to easily. I was finding my new mount a real joy to ride.

Early in my relationship with Rocky, I surprised myself by venturing out of the safe, small arena and into the expanse of paddocks. If anything were going to go awry with this powerful horse, an open field would be the place, so this decision pushed me beyond my comfort zone. At some level, I recognized this trait as one that had driven me all my life, the very urging that put me back on my feet and that had me cast my wheelchair aside. Rising to a challenge would prove to be a source of my strength as I faced the struggles in our family life, too.

I whispered in Rocky's ear as I opened the paddock gate and climbed back in the saddle. "You'll look after me, won't you, boy?"

The paddock stretched out boundless in front of us—no fences in sight, only open field to the horizon. My heart pumped as I gingerly pushed Rocky into a gentle trot. *Come on, Janine. You can do more than this.* I squeezed my inside leg at the girth, moving my outside leg back slightly. Rocky responded by breaking into his rhythmic, comfortable canter. With a knot in my stomach, I lifted myself out of the saddle and adjusted my posture to what seemed like a more natural way to sit as we went uphill.

I was in for a surprise. With no weight on his back, ex-racehorse Rocky took my rise from the saddle as his green light to gallop, something he had done countless times with jockeys. But of course I wasn't a jockey; in fact, I had never sat atop a horse running at full speed. Instinctively, I grabbed the reins solidly, gripped my knees tightly to his sides, and leaned my weight into his stride.

Reaching the top of the rise, I pulled back on the reins. "Whoa, boy!" I cried. Rocky instantly transitioned to a canter, then a trot, and before long, I was sitting back in the saddle as I walked him out.

What a rush! I stroked his neck, barely able to contain my excitement and full of appreciation for this wonderful animal. Just weeks earlier, I had been scared of even sitting on such a huge horse; now I was galloping across open paddocks with sheer joy and abandon, trusting him completely. Our playful jaunts around the farm became a regular thing for Rocky and me, a refreshing digression from the structured dressage training and a welcome escape from Tim's mercurial behavior.

A deepening love and respect for Rocky was unavoidable. He was a gorgeous horse, who instinctively kept watch over me. Over the next few years, he would teach me so much more than riding. Neither of us knew it yet, but Rocky was going to get me through some tough times and over many hurdles—literally and in life. He would prove to be, indeed, my Rock of Gibraltar.

› 28 ‹

Around this time, I began to experience debilitating migraines. At first, I put it down to the flu, but when they persisted for several weeks and compromised my sleep, I began to worry that something with my health might be amiss. More than a year had passed since Tim had first taken sick leave from the airline, and he'd spent most of that time in bed. Trying to juggle the demands of a husband who was unwell, three small children, the farm (with all its upkeep and animals), and my speaking career was taking a toll on both my physical and emotional well-being.

At times I felt Tim was slipping away from his family, that all I could do was wait patiently for his return. But gauging by his mood swings, I had no idea when that might be. As much as I tried to protect the kids from Tim's struggles and to maintain some semblance of a normal home life, I knew they sensed all was not well.

Suddenly and without warning, Tim went missing. I came home from dropping the kids at school and noticed his car was gone, which was unusual. I tried to reach him on his cell phone, but it was turned off. At first I assumed the best-case scenario: he had gone fishing down the coast, which he loved to do, and had probably forgotten his phone in the car. By late afternoon, there was still no word. He knew I had a commitment to travel to Sydney for a speaking engagement and that I'd arranged to have a babysitter for the night. So I felt confident my husband would consider that and be back by the time I got home that evening.

As it happened, Tim stayed away, incommunicado, for five full days, with each passing day increasing the feeling of dread that something terrible had happened. When he finally turned up safe, there was no mention of his having gone AWOL. This proved to be the start of a pattern I found deeply unsettling.

The unpredictability of his behavior made it increasingly impossible for me to help him manage his illness. For example, once I returned home from taking the kids to school to find that our outdoor furniture had been thrown in the pool, along with a bag of my clothes. The kitchen trash bin lay on the ground with rubbish strewn all over the floor. Some of the cupboard doors were missing, ripped right off the hinges. The house and grounds were a complete mess.

I found Tim sitting on the steps, his head on his knees, pieces of broken plates on the ground at his feet. My stomach in knots, I tried talking to him, but he had nothing to say. He looked dejected, as if he had lost all hope. I wanted desperately to help, to offer some solace, but it appeared that nothing could drag him out of his dark place.

When he wasn't sleeping or missing on walkabout, Tim spent his days in the back shed, working on a variety of projects, none of which seemed to get finished. During his time spent there, Tim had reconfigured the shed into a virtual second home, with a fireplace, a fridge, and even a television.

Curiously, in that environment he was social, and our shed soon became a second home to his mates. In the afternoon, after they had clocked off work, numerous guys from the neighborhood would come around and consume copious amounts of beer with Tim. He and his buddies would often hang out there until the wee hours of the morning, watching soccer matches or whatever else was on television.

When I would wander up to check on my husband, I'd have to make my way through discarded beer cans and cigarette butts, not to mention scraps of building materials scattered about like so much junk. Finding the condition of the shed deplorable and worrying all the more about Tim's state of mind, I tried in vain to raise the subject with him. He'd either ignore me or turn and walk away without a word, both behaviors serving to further alienate me.

That shed became an obsession for Tim. The time he spent there mushroomed out of proportion to when he was at home with his wife and children. When he'd finally return to the house, it was always late, and he reeked of alcohol, which I detested. Many nights he didn't even bother coming back to the house at all.

His behavior grew increasingly erratic and unpredictable. There were times when he seemed to be firing on all cylinders, and on those days, I convinced myself that things had turned for the better. But no sooner than he'd have a good day, there'd be a sudden and striking deterioration in his health that put him right back in bed. I struggled to maintain my equilibrium, careful to avoid being sucked into that dark vortex with him, all the while trying to offer support but taking care to protect my children and myself.

As the intensity of Tim's mood swings escalated, it was apparent that his depression was taking a toll on my physical and emotional state. When my migraines persisted and I was no longer able to sleep, I decided it was time to show equal concern for my health. It was time to see my doctor.

"Janine, I think you are suffering from depression," she told me. Familiar with my complicated medical history, as well as what I had been going through with Tim, it was evident to her that I wasn't well. She went on to clarify my condition as reactive depression, a response to an event or circumstances that a patient finds traumatic. Any significant life challenges—the death of a loved one, the end of a relationship, losing or changing a job—could trigger it. Reactive depression, I learned, could come on after a single traumatic life event, or it could develop as a consequence of compiled disappointments or problems. Either way, I certainly qualified as a candidate.

At her suggestion, I began therapy. It felt good to be able to sit down and safely talk to someone about what was happening and to develop strategies to cope. Although at first hesitant to admit it, I recognized that at times I no longer wanted to be in the marriage. Thoughts like this triggered enormous guilt, but it was only prudent that we explore my options if circumstances at home did not improve. Equally important, we considered how best to look after myself during the fearsome times of Tim's increasingly violent outbursts. They were not a cure-all, but these sessions with my therapist constituted the first steps in making some sense out of the confusion and instability at home.

As an adjunct to my therapy, I made it a priority most days to try to exercise. Being active not only helped to take my mind off everything; it also offered real physical benefits. I recalled from my university studies how exercise increases endorphins—the source of the often noted "runner's high"—and promotes good sleep. Perhaps best of all, regular and strenuous exercise helps to alleviate stress.

As a final step in managing my health, I joined a meditation group. The mindfulness skills we practiced taught me how to remain calm when life around me seemed chaotic, providing a respite from the uncertainty of life with Tim. Meditation offered me a safe haven, a place in my mind where I felt safe and supported. An unexpected benefit was that the practice also served as a palliative for many of the symptoms I had been experiencing of late: sadness, anxiety, irritability, stress, fatigue, and hopelessness.

Family and friends visited from time to time, many of them unaware of the upheaval going on behind closed doors. All the while, I maintained a state of denial, as if wishing it away could return our miracle of a family to the way we had been before Tim fell ill. What I failed to realize, though, was that the reality of it—and the attendant resentment, fear, and uncertainty—was slowly building up inside me, like a bomb with a slow-burning fuse.

I found myself growing increasingly angry, resentful that I had to carry the loads of both our young family and the labor on our farm. I felt lonely and often burst into tears out of pure frustration for the seemingly hopeless situation of my life. I tried to hide my anguish from the kids as best I could. There were many days when after dropping them off at school, I would sob uncontrollably all the way home in the privacy of my car.

Our once tidy, cozy house now looked more like a battle zone, with broken dishes and holes in the walls from where Tim had punched his fist in a fit of rage or frustration. I was constantly on guard and worried for our children's safety, intimidated by Tim's mood swings, and deathly afraid of doing or saying something to upset him.

Obviously, the relationship with my husband had suffered greatly, both physically and emotionally. We'd long since lost the ability to communicate at any meaningful level, and as we gradually drifted apart, it became difficult to connect with even a modicum of intimacy. Tim's struggles aside, I needed to let him know that I, too, was having a difficult time. It seemed that whenever I tried to talk about my needs or about us, he would either shrug it off and ignore me or, worse, raise his voice and storm out in a rage. I felt an overwhelming sense of loss for what we'd had and for what might never be regained. My "dream come true" had turned into a nightmare. The sadness of that realization hung like a pall over our once happy home.

Apart from my speaking engagements, I seldom socialized. Whenever I received an invitation to an event, I found the easiest way out was to make up an excuse and politely decline, which I did frequently. I didn't have the courage or the energy to attempt to discuss what was going on at home, the details of which were far too intimate and, for me, too shameful to share. Eventually and predictably, invitations were less frequent once people became accustomed to my turning them down.

A crushing outcome of the demands of trying to hold all these things together was the effect it had on my riding, my sole source of solace. The combined pressure of training to competitive standards while looking after my family and home ultimately became too much. Reluctantly, I made the heartbreaking decision to let go of my dream of competing with Rocky in the Paralympics. I packed my saddle and riding gear away in the tack room, not knowing when I'd next have the chance to use them. Then I bid a tearful goodbye to my Rock of Gibraltar; he returned to his original home, where he was retired.

Yet again, it felt like my dreams and aspirations were being snatched from me. This time, however, it wasn't at the hands of a reckless driver but by my own husband's baffling and debilitating illness.

As it turned out, neither Rocky nor I would ever compete in dressage again.

I lived two distinctly different lives: the public one I'd popularized in my inspirational books and speaking engagements and the deeply dark and fearful secret one at home. Ironically, I still received letters from people who found motivation in my story and who told me how pleased they were that I had found happiness with Tim after all the losses I'd endured. *How could I possibly tell them that my life had become a complete mess? That I struggled to get by and was deeply unhappy? That Tim and I no longer had the blissful marriage they'd read about in my books or seen portrayed in TV interviews? What if they knew that my current tragedies rivaled those I'd suffered with my accident?*

As is so often the case when life is about to take a dramatic turn, the galvanizing event for change came unexpectedly. One day, while Tim and I were both working in our office, he slammed his fist down on the computer keyboard in a pique of frustration. A stream of profanity followed. He grabbed his coffee mug and hurled it at the monitor, shattering the cup into tiny pieces. By now I'd learned to recognize these symptoms straightaway: he was going through a low episode, and we needed to do something about it immediately.

"Tim, I think you should phone the doctor," I said, hopeful that medical intervention would stave off potentially more dangerous depressive outbursts.

Instead, my suggestion enraged him further. "No! Why don't *you* fucking ring him?" he yelled. "Maybe *you* need some help!"

After his tantrum subsided, Tim announced that he was leaving for a month to go fishing in northern Queensland. I was flabbergasted and demoralized. It was the middle of winter. We had no wood stocked, and the cattle needed to be hand-fed daily. Once again, I would be left alone with the demands of the farm and kids, all the while juggling the career I relied on to keep the household and family financially afloat.

As I watched Tim drive away, I wondered how in the world I was going to get through the next month on my own. Then I realized that I had felt and been alone for such a long time now anyway that his absence ultimately wouldn't have much of an impact. In that instant, a wave of calm certainty washed over me: I knew beyond doubt that there was nothing more I could do. I was confident that no matter how much I wanted to help Tim get better, to *make* him better, it was beyond my ability to do so. There was a time to hold on and a time to let go. I had done everything possible to help Tim, but now it became clear that the only person able to help Tim was Tim.

As it turned out, while he was away, the children and I enjoyed the respite from his mood swings, which had so long dominated our lives. Our house became a home once more, alive with laughter and spontaneity. Music filled the household, and the kids made as much noise as they wanted without fear of reprimand. We delighted in this glimpse of normality, a reprieve that I (and I suspected the children) didn't want to end.

All along I'd managed to convince myself that the way we had been living was acceptable. Now I realized that it wasn't. I still hoped against hope for Tim's full recovery, but it was clear that this wouldn't happen by enduring the status quo. I had come to the absolute limit of all my emotional and physical resources. As I saw it, neither Tim nor I was going to survive if our lives together continued this way. Pushing emotion aside, I made the decision to leave, even as my heart ached for what would be lost forever. I feared what might lie ahead but was determined to do what I had to do for the sake of my children, and myself.

⟩ 29 ⟨

In my heart, I knew I couldn't have done any more to save my marriage. The breakup with Tim and the loss of a happy home proved a difficult and challenging time, one that in many ways was even harder for me to bear than my accident.

By the time my divorce was final, I had been speaking professionally for more than twenty years, presenting to a wide range of audiences, from twenty people in a boardroom to twenty thousand at the Melbourne Tennis Centre. Although I loved my work as a motivational speaker, my abiding priority remained caring for my children. I had wanted to give them the experience of living on the land, growing up feral and free, as I liked to put it. On the farm, their lives were filled with outdoor adventure and play, a unique perspective that I hoped would serve them well later in life. I wanted to give them as much stability in their upbringing as I could, even though at times I was stretched emotionally, physically, and financially. I valued watching them grow up and knew that our time together would pass quickly. Sometimes I tried too hard and, like any parent, fumbled terribly, but I consoled myself in remembering that I always strived to do the best I could under the challenging circumstances.

There have been countless instances over the years when I have questioned my own behavior and revisited my decisions. I am comforted when I see the young adults my children have become. Each of them is loving, caring, and empathetic, characteristics that might have developed not in spite of everything they went through but because of it. My children have taught me so much about resilience and adaptability, skills I am happy to see in their life toolkits as well as mine.

Unbeknownst to me, life was about to put me through an experience that would test my abilities in resilience and acceptance yet again. The global financial crisis that began in 2008 with subprime mortgages in America created ripples around the world. But it never crossed my mind that it would have such profound effects on my own life or the small country town in Australia where I lived.

The first sign of that impact was the decline in requests for speaking engagements—not just for me but also for all my associates on the speaking circuit. As companies began to feel the pinch of a shrinking economy, outside speakers for their conferences were perceived as a luxury they could do without.

As my bookings first declined, I wasn't too concerned. I took small loans on my home as needed to cover the shortfall in my income, a palliative measure that reflected my sanguine view of the slowdown. As time passed with less and less work though, I began to get concerned about my mounting debt. To address that, I decided to put my house on the market. I reckoned that when it sold I would pay off my debt, buy a smaller place, and still be able to support my kids through the remainder of their schooling.

It turned out I wasn't the only one with this idea. It seemed there were more sellers wanting to downsize than buyers looking to move up. Nobody wanted a large house like mine, with lots of land, and the small enclave I lived in was hit especially hard. People caught in the meltdown began losing their homes, along with their accrued equity and much of their savings. As sellers were forced to take offers well below value or for far less than their mortgages, the market fell off a cliff.

A full two years after I put my house on the market, it still hadn't sold, and I was seriously worried. Despite my continually lowering the price, no offers were forthcoming. My monthly payments were increasing, as I borrowed more just to stay afloat. It wasn't long before this cycle put me in a position in which I didn't just *want* to sell but now *had* to sell.

In 2012, I finally sold the house, for less than half of what I'd paid. It was the only offer I had during the entire time it had been on the market. I had no choice but to accept it. Once I paid out my mortgage and the loans I'd taken out to survive, I was left with nothing. I was devastated. The cruel reality was that not even a home I had so carefully tended could offer me a true sense of security.

In the days before the sale was to close, I sat on my back porch trying to digest what had gone wrong. *How could this have happened?*

What could I have done differently? What am I going to do now? My emotions vacillated from anger to disbelief to fear and finally to despair. The bitterest pill to swallow was that I felt like I had let my children down, knowing how much they loved our home.

At one point, Annabel came into my bedroom to find me sitting in my corner chair crying. "Mum, what's wrong?" she asked.

"I'm so sorry, sweetheart," I said sobbing. "I know how much you love our home, and I'm not sure where we are going to move to now."

She sat down beside me. "Mum, don't worry. It's going to be okay," she said. "You have given us everything, and I'm so grateful that we had the opportunity to live in such a beautiful place." She put her arms around me and gave me an enormous hug. "It's just a house. It's not that important. We'll find something else, but at least we still have each other."

Then in her usual funny manner, she imparted a pearl of wisdom that belied her twenty-one years. "You know, I think life is like a game of Monopoly. Sometimes you win; sometimes you lose," she said as she laughed.

Through my tears, I laughed, too. Annabel was right. That was the gift in all of this: no amount of money or anything else material could take away from what really mattered, and that was the love my children and I felt for one another. Reacting to fear and stress, I had placed too much importance on something external—a house—and that was never meant to be as enduring as my family.

› 30 ‹

During this time, one of the most remarkable events of life on my own started with a meeting. I was sitting in a coffee shop at Sydney Airport, waiting for someone I had yet to meet in person. Mike Lundgren was the curator for TEDx Kansas City, Missouri—a branch of the widely popular, punchy TEDTalks, featuring "Ideas Worth Spreading." Mike had been working in Australia for the past month, and we had arranged to meet before his flight back to the United States.

I had been put in contact with Mike via my newly engaged American literary agents, Jo-lynne Worley and Joanie Shoemaker, both his longtime friends. When I mentioned to them that I had long harbored the ambition to do a TED talk, they connected me with Mike without hesitation.

"If you want some advice on TED, Mike's the one to talk to," they told me. "He put Brené Brown on the map with her talk a few years ago." I had already watched her TEDx talk, "The Power of Vulnerability," which I loved, so it was with great excitement that I awaited my appointment with Mike.

My extensive public speaking experience and numerous life lessons notwithstanding, I didn't know what my "idea worth spreading" would be. My typical keynote address covered so many subjects; it would be hard to pick only one. Adding to my consternation was the TED talk time factor. My usual presentation spanned an hour, so how would I compact my story into TEDx's eighteen-minute limit?

As I waited, I took a moment to reflect on the myriad aspects of my adulthood thus far, starting with my accident and recovery as obvious key events that shaped my life. I thought about learning to fly, becoming an aerobatics instructor, meeting Tim, and starting the family I'd always dreamt I'd have. Then I lost my loving husband to a devastating illness and was forced to continue raising three children as a single mother. I'd watched helplessly as my marriage unraveled, taking with it our happy home. Along the way, I'd published four more books after

Never Tell Me Never and gained international acclaim as a motivational speaker. I'd bought a lovely home after we left the farm, then lost it to the worldwide financial meltdown. Yes, I had plenty of gritty stories to share, but which *one* idea could I share that TEDx audiences would find most compelling?

My thoughts were interrupted as I recognized Mike walking toward me.

"Hi, Janine," he said as he opened his arms to hug me. "It's so great to finally meet you."

"It's great to meet you, too, Mike." I returned his embrace with equal enthusiasm.

I understood that Mike was meeting me to determine if something in my story would be worthy of a coveted invitation to Kansas City, one of the more prestigious TEDx venues. Realizing what was at stake in this interview, I had worked up a good case of nerves ahead of our meeting, but Mike's charm and warmth instantly put me at ease. Over a cup of coffee, I learned that Jo-lynne and Joanie had given Mike some of my background, although he had yet to read any of my books. I assumed he would prefer a real-time exchange to help him decide if my story was TEDx-worthy and to allow him to gauge my storytelling skills.

Mike listened intently as I recalled the details of my accident and for the first time shared the experience of leaving my body, something I had previously felt uneasy putting into words. He took it all in and paused reflectively. "So, what would you say are some of the most important lessons you learned since your recovery?" he asked.

Chatting with Mike, I realized that despite so many challenges, the time after my accident was rich and full of many key lessons. Apart from the gifts of my children and my friends, I had the good fortune to travel to so many interesting destinations, meeting so many wonderful characters through my speaking engagements. As often as not, it was a chance meeting that moved me further along the journey of healing—from the cab driver in Melbourne who insisted on giving me his cherished prayer beads to the reformed ex-convict whose bracelet I wore with pride and grace.

"But, Janine, if you could narrow it down to just one most valuable lesson, what would that be?" Mike asked again, with added emphasis.

Thus challenged, I thought about the physical burdens I had endured since my accident, some visible—like the deformity of my legs—and some less so—like my continued dependence on a catheter. I remembered how I had felt so self-conscious about my atrophied calves after the initial recovery from my accident that I visited a plastic surgeon to inquire about implants. What I realized now was that in my overwhelming gratitude for being able to walk again, I had forgotten all about my withered calves. Not only did the opinion of others no longer matter, but I was proud of the ability of my little chicken legs, as I took to calling them, to support and transport me. And it was then that the answer to Mike's question—my one most compelling life lesson—dawned on me.

"Mike," I began slowly but with confidence, "I think the single most important lesson I have learned from the whole of my life experiences is that I am not my body."

Beaming, Mike pointed at me and declared emphatically, "Now, *that* is a TED talk!"

› 31 ‹

After numerous emails with Mike, culminating in a draft of my planned talk for his review, I was invited to present at TEDx Kansas City, with a scant four months to prepare. On the TEDx website, novelist Amy Tan describes the preparation for her TED talk as "something that creates a near-death experience, but near death is good for creativity." I had been given another potentially life-changing opportunity, and along with it, a lot of work to do in precious little time.

The theme for this TEDx was "The Long View," and the venue was the Kauffman Center for the Performing Arts, a stunning state-of-the-art facility in Kansas City. The conference would be held in the elegant Helzberg Hall, a performance auditorium that seats sixteen hundred people and provides acoustics befitting the world's best musical and theatrical productions.

The brief from Mike was this: the TEDx audience is sophisticated, engaged, and intelligent. They get it, and they get it quickly. In addition to those who would hear my talk live, there would be many thousands—perhaps even millions—more who would view my talk once it was posted online. He then sent me a summary of "The TED Commandments," a checklist for presenters. Reading these guidelines, along with numerous other coaching articles Mike sent me, I knew I had my work cut out for me. I decided I'd begin by writing the most powerful and succinct TED-worthy talk I could deliver. I vowed to myself that for the next sixteen weeks, I was going to live and breathe TED, and nothing else.

When I mentioned my upcoming talk to the producer of *Never Tell Me Never*, David Elfick, he suggested I reach out to a friend of his, acting coach Dean Carey. Dean was the founder and creative director of Actors Centre Australia (ACA), a world-class dramatic arts training facility—the very place where fellow Aussie Hugh Jackman launched his acting career. I called Dean straightaway and left a message for him.

Once Dean and I connected, we chatted non-stop for over an hour. He was open, warm, and as excited as I about the prospect of helping me hone my TED presentation. I sent him emails outlining my ideas, and the following week, I traveled to meet with him in person. From that time on, Dean and I rehearsed and prepared as a team—with as much commitment and diligence as I would have had with any of my athletic coaches. He was full of passion for what I was trying to achieve, and he wholeheartedly believed in the value and power of my "I am not my body" message. When not meeting in person, we chatted on a near-daily basis, following up with constant volleys of emailed thoughts and ideas. Every few weeks, I would travel to the ACA studio, where we'd rehearse and fine-tune my presentation live, on Dean's ACA stage.

The overarching theme of my talk was the proverbial hero's journey, loosely based on the work of Joseph Campbell. I had been tinkering with the idea of using a simple folding chair to symbolize a wheelchair, but ultimately that idea morphed into one of having a series of chairs on stage, each representing a distinct segment of my journey. We staggered the chairs to represent my setbacks and progress along the way and to reflect the struggles and breakthroughs as well.

Working with Dean was a delightful, if demanding, experience. He pushed me to take risks and to be vulnerable and real on stage—and to operate outside of my comfort zone. Often I took certain parts of my story for granted, but Dean perceived their significance and encouraged me to share these more intimate aspects of my journey. One day as we were workshopping ideas, I offhandedly mentioned the exercise nurse, Wayne, and what the entire spinal ward had done with connecting straws. Dean jumped to his feet, visibly excited. "That is an amazing story! We have to incorporate it in your talk!" Though the straw story was something I'd never shared with an audience before, it reflected a message we agreed would be a vital part of my presentation. With Dean's insight, "connection" became a central theme of my talk—and one we chose to be represented by one of my six chairs. From there, we settled on themes for each of the remaining chairs on the stage:

Chair One: Who I Was
Chair Two: Who I Became
Chair Three: Connection
Chair Four: Bargaining and Acceptance
Chair Five: Freedom
Chair Six: I Am Not My Body

As the day of my performance drew near, Dean and I began to rehearse with "real-time" practices at his ACA center. Before the start of each run-through, we would set up my chairs exactly as they would be on the TEDx stage. We drilled down relentlessly and meticulously on each chair's message, assessing the value of every single word in my address. My preparation wasn't limited to ACA rehearsals, though. I arranged my dining chairs to mimic the TEDx stage, and I would run through my talk for whichever friends and family were willing to play audience in my home.

Countless run-throughs and edits later, Dean and I were at last happy with the final version of my presentation. He then organized a complete dress rehearsal in front of his acting students, a test of my readiness that proved both invaluable and inspiring. I was as ready as I'd ever be.

› 32 ‹

Upon arriving in Kansas City, I participated in the TEDx dress rehearsal and met some of the other speakers. I found the auditorium in which I'd be presenting to be even more impressive than I expected. When I looked out from the stage to the hundreds of empty seats, my stomach churned with excitement, anticipation, gratitude—and nerves!

The following day, I sat in a dressing room, downstairs in the labyrinth beneath the Kaufman Center, awaiting the call from the staff that the program was nearing my turn. As I prepared to go onstage, audience members were starting to arrive and pick up their goody bags, which included a drinking straw to accompany my presentation.

In my dressing room, I glanced at my phone and saw a text message from Dean. It read: "Breathe the auditorium in, trust each chair, have full permission to be it all, and share it all. Everyone is tucked under your heart." Heeding Dean's wise counsel, I closed my eyes and collected my thoughts and intentions.

On the monitor in my dressing room, I watched the speakers who preceded me. When it was my turn, I headed backstage to have my microphone fitted. I recognized a familiar feeling in my stomach, a knot of nerves and excitement that always came just before I took the stage. I reminded myself of my meticulous preparation, that I was ready. I was focused and calm. I heard Mike introduce me. I closed my eyes, took a breath, and said a silent prayer.

As I made my way behind the row of chairs arranged on the stage, I placed my hand on the first chair. Standing there, I looked out toward the audience and saw . . . *nothing!* The spotlights aimed to focus attention on my chairs were so blinding that I couldn't even make out the first row. More alarming, I couldn't see the clock that had been placed onstage to help me keep track of time. *Stay calm.* I knew I had rehearsed this talk enough to cast aside these small issues, and I assumed my familiar starting-line focus.

I remembered what Dean had shared with me during our rehearsal: "Before you speak the first word, pause and take a moment to look out toward each section of the audience. Acknowledge every person, and silently give thanks to each one for being there." I did as he instructed, and then began with the words, "Life is about opportunity . . ."

Surrounded by blackness and complete silence, I made my way through and around my chairs, as I invited each person to share my journey. It no longer mattered that I couldn't see because I could sense every person in the hall. It was an extraordinary and magical experience.

As I neared the end of my talk, I reached into my back pocket for my straw. I stumbled slightly in the darkness but managed to stay on my feet. Suddenly, I heard an incredible and distracting rumbling in my headsets. *What is that? Has my mike stopped working? Is it a signal that I've gone over my allotted time?* I walked into the blackness toward the front of the stage, grasping my straw, and resumed speaking.

"We are all connected by millions and millions of straws . . . we need to join them up, and we need to hang on if we are to move toward our collective bliss. It is now time to shed our focus on the physical and embrace the virtues of the heart." I paused and then lifted my straw, inviting the audience to do the same.

"So raise your straws if you'll join me!"

I took a step out of the spotlight that had blinded me for the entire presentation. Adjusting my gaze, I saw the entire audience rise to their feet, and thousands of outstretched arms with straws held high. I was flooded with gratitude. *Thank you.* I said it over and over in my mind, as I looked out at the sea of straws.

Thank you, not just for the experience of being here tonight but for the struggles, the breakthroughs, the losses, and the triumphs. Thank you.

› EPILOGUE ‹

As the global financial crisis passed and I began speaking more regularly again, I managed to save enough to put a deposit down on a small cottage, not far from the two-acre property I lived in before. Though a fraction of the size of our former house and in need of repair, I made sure it felt like home for me, and my children.

Annabel returned after years of traveling overseas, competing on the freestyle ski circuit. Representing Australia on the Olympic team came to a sudden and dramatic end when she suffered a torn knee ligament, just six weeks out from the 2014 Sochi Winter Games. It was a heartbreaking loss for her. She had already received her Olympic jersey, and she had trained relentlessly to be in top competitive form for her events. Annabel handled the setback graciously, seeming to shrug it off without lament. One day, after the surgery repairing her ligament, I asked her why she didn't seem devastated. Without hesitating, she replied, "Because I have been watching you my whole life, Mum." After years of hurtling herself over enormous jumps, skiing at breakneck speed over all sorts of obstacles, Annabel decided to retire from ski competition and return to university studies to complete her degree in psychology.

Charlotte was accepted to medical school, requiring a move to Melbourne. I wondered if it was my accident that led her into that field. Had living with a mother who was in and out of the hospital her entire life seeped into Charlotte's consciousness, culminating in her desire to become a doctor?

Angus, while still in high school, had moved in with his father the previous year. Although this took some getting used to, I recognized it as an important step for him. It was his time to cross the bridge from adolescence to young adulthood, and it seemed Angus wanted his dad to play a more hands-on role in his life.

My dad suffered a stroke in 2011, the same day Annabel was having her knee surgery. The effects were immediately devastating and ultimately unrecoverable. Debilitating paralysis and significant impairment in many abilities meant he was confined to a nursing home for what would prove to be the remainder of his days. After five long months in bed, suffering from ulcerated bedsores and numerous other indignities in his struggle, Dad barely clung to life. I sensed that he was hanging on out of obligation as the guardian and provider for his family.

I took his hand in mine, just as he'd done for me in the ICU so many years earlier, and I consoled him: "Dad, you offered me your strength when I needed it, and you saved my life. I'm okay now and so is Mum, so it's alright if you're ready to leave."

He passed in his sleep not long after. He was a wonderful, kind, loving father, and I miss him terribly.

Mum still lives in her beach house north of Sydney, where she leads an active and full life, playing tennis regularly and socializing with her friends. I'll never forget her unwavering support and strength during my ordeal and recovery. As a mother myself, I cannot to this day fathom how much pain she endured on my behalf.

Uncle Darryl, the upbeat orderly who gave me playful gowns and was a source of tireless consolation to our family (especially my dad) while I was in spinal, took his own life. I was told he had been diagnosed with incurable cancer.

Maria, the young accident victim with whom I shared the spinal ward, finally left her body in 2014. As a high-level quadriplegic, she had remained dependent on around-the-clock care for all of her most basic needs throughout her life. Maria and I stayed in contact and spoke often over the years, during which time I never once heard her complain about her life, the single quality of hers most often mentioned by friends and family, and one I hold as saintly. Always smiling, Maria was the bravest person I will ever know, an inspiration to me, and to so many others. She gave me the most precious gift in life: the gift of acceptance.

Boggie, the Royal Australian Air Force pilot who introduced me to aerobatics, was out on a search-and-rescue mission when the single-engine plane he was flying had a catastrophic mechanical failure. The engine seized and coated the windscreen with oil. Unable to see, and gliding over unlandable terrain with no power, he valiantly gave it his best, trying to gently settle the crippled aircraft onto the tree-tops in the dense bush below. Boggie and his copilot, along with several passengers, perished in the crash.

Dr. Stephen, the brilliant orthopedic surgeon whose delicate operation saved my spinal cord and rebuilt my vertebra, is still widely regarded as one of Australia's most prominent practitioners in the field. Even now on his mantel is a framed photo of me, suited up and ready for a special F18 flight I had with the Royal Australian Air Force—a touchstone for him of a particularly successful outcome for one of his special patients.

Dr. Blum, the equally talented neurosurgeon who painstakingly picked shards of bone from my spinal cord, has since retired from private practice and is now working as a medical consultant.

Ado left orthopedics soon after I was discharged, to specialize in emergency response medicine, initially working for the helicopter medevac company that flew me from the scene of my accident. He enjoyed a stint in the United States as a field physician for the popular reality show *Survivor*, after which he returned to his homeland. He has since founded a company called NeckSafe, which develops and promotes spinal-cord stabilization implements and techniques for first responders. Ado and I share a unique bond that was forged in acute spinal, and we remain dear friends.

Finally, a touching testament to the serendipity with which my life has been blessed is worth noting. There's a special relationship that developed between the only person who witnessed my accident and me. Elizabeth was driving behind the truck that struck me. She covered me with a blanket and held my hand until medical help arrived. Shortly thereafter, she penned a poem that captured her feelings from that terrible day. She mailed it to the hospital, not yet knowing if I had survived. Much later, as a pilot, I flew to an airport near her rural home to thank her. Our reunion was, for her, both startling and delightful, given how I appeared when she last saw me sprawled on the roadside. We discovered we had the same birthday, a coincidence that keeps us in touch at least once a year.

For the first time in my entire life, I was living alone, in my cottage. I had been a single mum for more than ten years, in a vibrant and lively environment, so it was strange to wake up to an empty house. I was recovering after yet more surgery, this time a hysterectomy, and could feel the internal stitches pulling every time I moved. The required break from exercise made me lethargic and vulnerable. I felt an overpowering sense of my aloneness.

With the day's first cup of tea in my hand, I sat at my desk and opened my computer. There was a message waiting for me from one of the million-plus who had seen my TEDx talk. TED corporate had selected my presentation to be featured on their main website—once it was even featured as the talk of the day. Ever since, I had been flooded with emails and messages from around the world. Viewers from places as far away as the Himalayas, Saudi Arabia, Egypt, and a small, remote village in Colombia all wrote to let me know how my message had touched them. This morning's email came from India:

> Dear Miss Shepherd,
> Thank you for sharing your wonderful life. I want you
> to know that for the past nineteen years, I have been
> fighting an ailment, and it has affected my day-to-day
> life. It has become so bad that for the past weeks I have
> been contemplating suicide. But today after seeing
> and listening to you, I have a new ray of hope. Pray I
> succeed, too. My journey begins NOW.

As I reread the words on the screen, I tried to digest the enormity of what this gentleman had written. I knew then that even sitting in my home by myself, I was never truly alone. Like that metaphor with the straws, we are all connected by and through our stories. I was reminded how important it is that we reach out to one another and continue to share our respective lessons and discoveries, for this reason if no other.

As I looked back over the landscape of my life and the many setbacks I had endured, I saw that every loss had also offered a gift, even if I hadn't recognized it at the time. Whenever I was called upon to loosen my grip on some cherished part of my life, I was consequently given the opportunity to start again, to create anew something of value. The way I now saw it, every ending carried the seeds of possibility, a chance to start over. Experience had underscored for me the wisdom of Lao Tzu's words, "When I let go of what I am, I become what I might be." And it reminded me that, like the man who wrote to me from India, my journey, too, begins now.

I had reached yet another seminal moment in my life. My children were now young adults, off living their own lives. In many ways, I had done what I needed to do in Australia and now thought it was time to move on, to spread my wings. And so I found myself on the cusp of a decision that, once made, would radically alter the course of my life: I considered a move to America.

When I first hinted at this potential change, I got a predictable range of responses. My kids thought my idea was an "awesome adventure," even as they knew we would all miss one another terribly. Many friends and some of my family thought I was crazy. "You don't know anyone there. Where will you live?" Mum asked. "What will you do for work?" I did my best to assuage her fears by telling her I knew at least, well, four Americans.

My decision made, within a matter of weeks I had set things irrevocably in motion. I put my house up for rent, hoping to cover the mortgage until such time when I returned. I applied for a US work visa; if granted, it would allow me to stay in the country for up to three years. I began to give away my furniture and household belongings. Some of it went to friends, while other pieces were donated to deserving charities. I did the same with most of my clothes. In the end, what I planned to bring to America would be just a few essential items, only so much as could fit in the compact car I'd buy once I settled into my yet-to-be-found new home.

Before I knew it, I was fastening my seat belt aboard an aircraft bound for the United States, ready to begin the next chapter of my life halfway across the world. Waiting to push back from the gate, I started chatting with the gentleman sitting next to me. He was dressed casually and had long hair, which made him look younger than I guessed him to be. Soon we were deep in conversation about our respective lives. He told me he was a lawyer but had only just returned to the profession after a long sabbatical.

"Why is that?" I asked.

"Well, I got into real estate development, building hospitals actually. I made an absolute fortune doing that, so I gave away my law practice," he began. "We lived the high life. My wife and I traveled first class everywhere, stayed in the best hotels. We owned vacation homes, expensive cars. We had everything we wanted."

"So what happened?"

"Well, during the global financial crisis, the construction industry crashed, and we lost it all," he said. "We ended up so broke, we didn't even have money for a cab ride. We moved into a rented house. My wife had to return to work, and I went back to practicing law."

"Wow, that's quite a story," I said. "So how do you feel about all that?"

Without hesitation, he replied in an even and heartfelt tone, "Actually, it's the best thing that ever happened to us. It was—still is—a gift."

I nodded my head and smiled, a gesture of understanding that needed no words.

I turned to look out my window. Absorbed in conversation, I hadn't yet noticed that we'd already taken off and climbed through a layer of cloud that was now fast disappearing beneath us. As far as I could see in every direction, we were immersed in a boundless blue sky. What better metaphor for life?

My thoughts drifted back to that terrible day so long ago, and the choice I made to return to my broken body. I was uncertain about where I was headed, the new direction my life would take, and what challenges were in store for me on that journey.

Now, as then, I am uncertain about where I am headed and what awaits me. And I still feel fear.

Yet I am not afraid.

› ACKNOWLEDGMENTS ‹

I want to start by acknowledging the hundreds of people who have written to me over the years, sharing their personal stories of loss and overcoming. Thank you for reminding me that I am never alone and how important it is that we continue to share our stories.

There are so many friends who have stood by me over the years, and I am grateful to each of them for the love and support that never wavers. Special mention goes to Mark Chambers and Lucy Palmer, who unfailingly read whatever I sent them, always offering helpful feedback and suggestions. Also, to my dear friend Annie Mackay for graciously offering me your home and hospitality whenever I return to Australia.

I am especially indebted to my soul sister, Indrani Goradia, whose first meeting with the "broken woman" was instrumental in getting my footing in the United States. Indrani, I am forever indebted to you for your generosity and kindness.

A shout out to my Ojai family: Jo and Byron, Cami and Jim, Kirsten, Jeff and Kate, Lucy, Molly, Nancy and Ray, Ron, and the whole hot-tub gang. Also, to my Rancho/Tahoe friends: Mike, Kimberly, Ron, Julie, Chelsea, and Hailey. To Libby Moore, Jen Hollingsworth, and Barbara Cogswell for your support throughout the years. And to Roman, Renee, Ben, and all my fellow PTTOWs for inviting me into the fold.

To my extraordinary literary agents and friends, Jo-Lynne Worley and Joanie Shoemaker. Thank you for your unwavering belief in my message, in me, and for never giving up on the search to find the perfect publisher for my story.

Mike Lundgren, TEDx curator for Kansas City: thank you for giving me the opportunity to share my story on the TED stage, the greatest platform for reaching a sophisticated world audience one could ever hope for. Thanks also to my talented and creative friend Dean Carey, founder of Actors Centre Australia, for tirelessly working alongside me in crafting my talk.

Special mention to Jono Fisher, founder of the Wake Up Project. I am honored to call you my friend.

My heartfelt thanks to Bruna Papandrea for inspiring the title.

I feel blessed to have teamed up with a publishing house with such integrity and heart, as evidenced in the work of every individual at Sounds True. Your respective and collective guidance helped me steer *Defiant* to its most authentic outcome. Thank you Haven Iverson, Jade Lascelles, Alice Peck, and Vesela Simic for your thoughtful comments in the revision process. To Mitchell Clute and Aron Arnold for guiding me through the most extraordinary experience while recording the audio version of this book. Tami Simon, a heartfelt thank you for inviting me into the Sounds True family.

I cannot begin to express how grateful I am to my family of origin: my mother, Shirley; my two sisters, Kim and Kelley; Morgan; and my "brother," Hap. (You too, Dad.)

As always, to my children: Annabel, Charlotte, and Angus. I know having a mum living overseas has been a strain at times, and although we all miss one another, I take solace in watching your lives unfold in the most exceptional way. I love you all dearly.

Finally, to my spiritual and writing partner, David, who collaborated with me every step along the way. Your love, support, and creative input have brought my story to life. While writing is a solitary process, I have been blessed to share this journey with you, and I am grateful for the extraordinary circumstances that brought us together. Your genius and gift for writing have improved every page. You inspire me to be the best writer, and person, I can be. None of this would be possible without you.

› ABOUT THE AUTHOR ‹

Janine Shepherd is an Australian author and internationally acclaimed inspirational speaker. A qualified commercial pilot and aerobatics flying instructor, she holds a bachelor's degree in human movement studies and education. Millions around the world have viewed her TEDx talk, "A Broken Body Is Not a Broken Person."

Janine is an ambassador for Spinal Cure Australia and has been awarded her country's highest civilian honor, the Order of Australia, for her service to the community, her inspiration, and her work in raising awareness of spinal cord research.

She is a mother to three children and now lives in Wyoming. Learn more about Janine and her work through her website, janineshepherd.com.

› ABOUT SOUNDS TRUE ‹

Sounds True is a multimedia publisher whose mission is to inspire and support personal transformation and spiritual awakening. Founded in 1985 and located in Boulder, Colorado, we work with many of the leading spiritual teachers, thinkers, healers, and visionary artists of our time. We strive with every title to preserve the essential "living wisdom" of the author or artist. It is our goal to create products that not only provide information to a reader or listener, but that also embody the quality of a wisdom transmission.

For those seeking genuine transformation, Sounds True is your trusted partner. At SoundsTrue.com you will find a wealth of free resources to support your journey, including exclusive weekly audio interviews, free downloads, interactive learning tools, and other special savings on all our titles.

To learn more, please visit SoundsTrue.com/freegifts or call us toll-free at 800.333.9185.

SOUNDS TRUE
many voices, one journey